THE SLEEPING GIANT AWAKENS
LEEDS UNITED 2016-17

T0315741

THE SLEEPING GIANT AWAKENS
LEEDS UNITED 2016-17

HEIDI HAIGH

HEIDI'S DEDICATION

I would like to dedicate this book to the fantastic worldwide Leeds United supporters. We have fans like Terje On Tour Hansen and Cato Visdal Mikalsen, both from Norway, who travel regularly to both home and away games. Other fans travel regularly from Sweden, Ireland and many countries from around the globe.

Fans from this country include Sue Evans, Carole Parkhouse, Margaret Clark, Keith Gaunt, Linda Smith, Karen Glynn, Gary Edwards and Mick Hewitt who I have stayed friends with ever since we met in the 1970s. There are too many more to mention by name, but I will always be grateful that we have our unique bond of following Leeds United and the loyalty and dedication of our fans are second to none!

Marching on Together!

First Published in Great Britain in 2017 by DB Publishing,
an imprint of JMD Media Ltd

© Heidi Haigh, 2017

All Rights Reserved. No part of this publication may be reproduced, stored in a retrieval system, or transmitted in any form, or by any means, electronic, mechanical, photocopying, recording or otherwise without the prior permission in writing of the copyright holders, nor be otherwise circulated in any form or binding or cover other than in which it is published and without a similar condition being imposed on the subsequent publisher.

ISBN 978-1-78091-567-8

Printed and bound in the UK

TABLE OF CONTENTS

FOREWORD

The bare statistics will forever say that the 2016–17 season saw Leeds United finish seventh in the Championship, five points short of a play-off position. Do the maths, and any football fan could reasonably deduce that 22 victories and 9 draws represented a decent effort which was unfortunate not to deliver a top six spot with a haul of 75 points. But that's not the real story. The figures do not do a remarkable campaign justice.

With her pen and camera Heidi Haigh's *The Sleeping Giant Awakens* reveals the true tale. Another close season of turmoil around LS11 followed by a low bar of expectation which was raised higher and higher before wobbling off its perch, could only be truly and accurately captured by one of those amazing supporters whose hopes were reignited before being dashed, along with tens of thousands of others come the following May. Heidi's knowledge and back catalogue of the history of watching her beloved club makes her a national footballing treasure. She is the epitomy of what it is to support Leeds United – unswerving loyalty despite regular heartbreak.

Adam Pope – Sports Broadcaster for the BBC

LEEDS UNITED SEASON PREVIEW

As I sit here today on Monday, 25 September, Leeds United sit proudly on top of the Championship, albeit on goal difference, and all could change by the time 10 p.m. comes tomorrow when they face third-place Cardiff City. Had you asked any Leeds United fan at the start of August where their team would lay in the table, if anyone had said top, I can bet a bottom dollar that they would have been kidding. What is even more remarkable is the fact that our former Head Coach jumped ship to join Championship rivals Middlesbrough in the summer, star striker Chris Wood wanted to try his luck in the Premiership at Burnley and three of last season's back five – Rob Green (to Huddersfield), Kyle Bartley (returned to Swansea) and Charlie Taylor (to Burnley) – all left the football club.

With Monk gone, new owner Andrea Radrizzani's first real task was to find a new Head Coach and he did this by appointing Thomas Christiansen, formerly of Apoel Nicosia. With the new boss in place, signings came in thick and fast and with Middlesbrough's former Head of Recruitment Victor Orta, Leeds made sixteen new signings. It's been a case of so far so good.

The season started with a hard-fought 3–2 win away at newly promoted Bolton Wanderers thanks to a brace from Kalvin Phillips and the last goal in a Leeds shirt for Chris Wood, before League Two side Port Vale were brushed aside 4–1 in the first round of the Carabao Cup, thanks to a hat trick from new signing Samuel Saiz. In doing so he became the first player to score a hat trick on his debut since Carl Shutt v. AFC Bournemouth in April 1989. Back-to-back goalless draws followed at home to Preston North End and Fulham respectively, before an impressive win at Sunderland thanks to goals from that man Saiz and a header from Stuart Dallas. Newport County came and went in the second round of the Carabao Cup with another hat trick, this time from Kemar Roofe, before an impressive start to the season continued with a 2–0 away win at Nottingham Forest.

Pierre Michel Lassoga came in from Hamburg as a direct replacement for Wood and marked his debut with a brace in a 5–0 win at home to Burton Albion. Leeds then topped the table for more than 24 hours for the first time since May 1990 with a hard-fought 2–0 win over Harry Redknapp's Birmingham City at Elland Road. A first defeat followed at bogey team Millwall, but the team bounced back with a penalty shoot-out win over Premier League Burnley at Turf Moor in the third round of the Carabao Cup. Last Saturday saw another hard-fought win, this time 3–2 at home to Ipswich Town, in which Lassoga scored his third goal for the club to keep the side top of the pile.

Just maybe, the good times are really just around the corner for all Leeds United fans. After all, it's been fourteen years since the likes of Arsenal, Chelsea, manchester united and Liverpool travelled to Elland Road to face the Whites in a league encounter and to me, that is a long time between drinks – and once this famous old club gets going, it really gets going!

Andrew Dalton – Freelance Sports Journalist

COMMENTS FROM FANS

WHO LOVE READING MY BLOGS AND SEEING MY PHOTOS!

As I do my blog for the fans, as a fan, I thought it was appropriate to use comments from those who enjoy reading my blogs for the Foreword, which I am very grateful for:

Warren Shepherd Always love your blogs Heidi. The detail you put into them is truly admirable. Couldn't be there today so enjoyed this read

Karen Cooper For all the tv pundits and newspaper reports your reports are the ones I look forward to. Always honest good or bad keep it up lady **Warren Shepherd** Yep unrivalled

Clive William Lewis Heidi great report. Thank you. What camera and lens are you shooting with. Terrific stuff all round. Clive from LA (originally born and raised in Moortown area).

Sean Caden You probably get this all the time Heidi, but I just wanted to thank you for what you are & what you do for Leeds United, both for the club & more importantly for the fans. Immeasurable contribution. X

Luke Duffy Just want to say thanks for your blogs. They are fantastic. I read all of them from Adelaide, Australia and actually makes me feel like I have been to Elland Road they have that much detail. Thanks again

Jody Cobb Another great blog Heidi. Personally I love the length of the posts. You can read bullet points on the beeb. Your blogs always read like they should, like a fan has written them ;) mot

Barbara Thomas I enjoy reading your blogs much more than the YEP reports, Heidi! I thought Leeds looked great on TV, but I also thought Sunderland were poor! Let's hope they learn to play like that at home now! MOT! 👍 ☺

Mark OB Great write up 👍

Tony Burtonshaw Fantastic. Thanks. I was there but love other accounts. Our start reminded me of our champions.. have a go don't let them settle.

Peter Sleigh Love it Heidi......a special day today.....

Kevin Raymond Jones Brilliant

Ian Donohue Brilliant read as always

Ilsf Andy Great report Heidi luv they just get better..

Peter Saunders Brilliant. Are you a journalist by any chance ??. MOT.

David Crosland Love reading your blog, brings a flavour of the game to us Spanish Whites. MOT.

Jeff Way Welcome back Heidi I am glad you had a good time and got back safe another great blog and I agree it is brilliant to see the sleeping giant waking up let's hope we keep it going all the way to next May MOT

Martyn Boyes Back to your best Heidi, love from Hong Kong

Brian Searson Cheers Heidi, welcome back, some of the football yesterday was awesome, can't wait to come up again on Tuesday for another instalment, actually bet on 5 nil so that's a couple of games paid for, take care, Brian, Falmouth whites.

Dave Williams Another great write up thanks Heidi. I listened to the game on LUTV and the stats showed that we really were dominant and played very well for 90 mins. Long may it continue! #MOT

Ian Donohue Brilliant read as always

Dave Luke Excellent write up again Heidi. I think they are getting better and better just like our team. Let's hope for another 3 points tomorrow.

Arnie Pirie So for Christmas iphone 8 and The Sleeping Gaint Awakens best sellers in UK

Liam Healy Thank you for posting every week. I ALWAYS look forward to you putting your pics up for 2 reasons... 1) they are quality 2) selfishly I always try to find myself. ALAW Honest, probably for the last 3 seasons I've looked through every pic it's a great service you provide and lufc should pay you accordingly 👓 You really do and it's down to people like yourself that selflessly do what you do that make me love our great club. So on behalf of me and my group we thank you very much x

Robert Taylor Love these stories of the mutual respect when Leeds fans meet up ! Do I need to say it ? - excellent report and you hit the nail on the head with so many comments. Thank you.

Paul Thompson Great blog that!! Always like reading yours.thanx Heidi m.o.t

Paul Broadbent Great blog. Love to read it 😊

Lynsey Elizabeth A great read Heidi. I'm really struggling to get away tickets this year so it's always good to read your match day blog. X

Rheinallt Bonoff Williams This is worthy of a Booker Prize...good read again 😊

Anthony John Mccann Love this page wafll on and on still top of championship MOT MARCHING ON TOGETHER"

PROLOGUE

After writing my books *Follow Me and Leeds United*, *Once a Leeds fan, always a Leeds fan* and my co-authored book with Andrew Dalton *The Good, The Bad and The Ugly of Leeds United*, I thought my writing days were at an end. It was only after the season 2016–17 had finished that I started to think that maybe I could write another book. As Leeds United had started stirring again and were awakening into a team that we as fans craved for, it made me realise that a good title for a book would be The Sleeping Giant Awakens. It is a phrase that has been used by many Leeds fans over the last season and I know there was a Facebook group with the title 'The Sleeping Giant has woken up' too. As I have been writing a blog for the last couple of seasons, which is published on my *Follow Me and Leeds United* page on Facebook and my website www.followmeandleedsunited. co.uk, many fans had asked me when I was writing another book? The blog is based on following Leeds United up and down the country plus any pre-season games I attended, and I have taken lots of photos along the way. Having then shared my experiences around the world with other Leeds United fan groups, the feedback I have got from them has been great. A few fans have even said that I make them feel as if they are there with me and I have a talent for doing this. What greater compliment can I have?

This got me thinking that maybe I should do another book based on my blog and include plenty of photos once again. This is based from a fan's perspective and takes you on a journey to all the games seen through my eyes. Many fans are regulars in my photos as they enjoy seeing themselves on my blog. All they have to do is ask, as I am always happy to oblige by taking photos. I am always happy for fans to share my photos too; all I ask is that they say that I took them. Although I am unable to put all the photos I have taken into a new book, they can all be found in the original blogs on the internet. To get in as many photos as possible, though, I have included lots in collages. Once again, on our journey throughout the year our fans have shown tremendous loyalty and have a great camaraderie so I wanted to share these memories with others.

After Garry Monk's appointment as manager (I'm a traditionalist and don't like to call him a coach!), it meant our pre-season once again had been late as far as preparations go. Our players were all getting used to one another at the start and initially once the season itself started we found ourselves in familiar territory in the lower half of the table. Once we ended up in the bottom three, many of us started to see relegation staring us in the face once again.

All of a sudden we managed to pull things round and creep away from the bottom of the table, which gave us hope that things were on the up. Instead of the usual noises that our season was going to be over in October once again, there was talk of aiming for the play-offs. Now that would be an achievement, especially as a 14th or 15th position in the table had been aspired to for a few seasons!

As the season went on, I actually started to enjoy my football once again and it was nice to see the team interacting with the fans. This is something that has been missing for a long time and the connection between us was something that the Leeds fans took to with gusto.

Although many fans thought the play-off position was secure as we neared the end of the season, personally I wanted to see us get as many points as we could and see where we were at the end. Sadly, by the time we played Burton away on 22 April 2017 we had dropped out of the top six and that put paid to any dreams of promotion. I still say that by putting out a weakened team at Sutton in the FA Cup, which meant we got beaten, would be pivotal. Winning breeds winning as far as I'm concerned and being the traditionalist that I am, the FA Cup will always mean something to me. To treat it with so much disregard by Garry Monk and the team was a disgrace. As far as I'm concerned the defeat had a big impact on the rest of the season and no matter what was going on behind the scenes at Elland Road, this was sacrilege!

Despite all this, though, the stirrings of how Leeds United can be if run properly are there to see. Crowds started flocking back, connecting the city to the club, and the one thing I love about it all, the atmosphere, was fantastic to be part of. I hope you enjoy the read as it takes you through the highs and lows of being a Leeds United fan. Marching on Together!

CHAPTER 1 – JULY 2016

SHAMROCK ROVERS, DUBLIN – 16 JULY 2016

Once again, I am going to write about my experiences of following Leeds United and take photos to show the journey. The fans who have enjoyed reading my experiences over the past couple of years have given me some great feedback, saying that they feel as if they are at the games with me. What better acknowledgement can I have?

My season started yesterday in Dublin when I decided I would go for the day. Many other Leeds fans took this option too although some, like my friend Sue, went on Mick Hewitt's trip and spent six days there returning home the day after the game. With Leeds also having a fantastic following of Irish fans there were obviously going to be lots of us there.

My day started at 4.15 a.m. when I woke up before my alarm went off and decided to just get up, as I was leaving the house in half an hour. After dropping my car in Guiseley I got a lift to the airport. I arrived at 6.00 p.m., and was surprised to see how many queues there were as soon as I got in the terminal. Luckily only having hand baggage, I went straight through very quickly and it was a very trouble-free process.

Although I was travelling on my own, I was meeting my friend in Dublin plus another couple of lads. One had brought my ticket for me as I had been experiencing difficulties when trying to

Shamrock Rovers 16.7.16

purchase one, and a big thank you goes to Paul Corrigan for doing this for me. The other wanted to buy my book *Follow Me and Leeds United*, so thank you Derek Mulligan for that!

I was stood in the queue for a coffee when I saw Danny Priestley and Gus from Bradford, so sat with them. There were a few other Leeds fans on the same flight including a lad from Sherburn who I recognised. It doesn't matter where I go, though, as there is always someone to talk to. It can be a complete stranger who comes up and starts talking about Leeds just because I'm wearing my Leeds things. Leeds fans everywhere.

After a good flight with Aer Lingus we arrived before 9.30 a.m. It was dark and dull as we got off the plane and I couldn't believe how nice it had been above the clouds. Hopefully the sun will come out later. One thing we had noted was how big Dublin airport was and how far we had to walk from one place to another. Danny and Gus got the bus to their hotel but helped me get the directions to where I could get the bus to Tallaght. I was stopping off halfway at the Interchange, the Red Cow Hotel, to get my ticket from Paul. Once I found the correct stop I asked about the bus and was told it would be about 20 minutes, so got a cup of tea. Saw the lad I knew from Sherburn (sorry I'm not great with names but know many by sight). I took a photo and told this other lad to get in it and they said he was a Newcastle fan. I said I don't mind I take anyone, meaning my photos. His response was something about being roasted, although not sure what he meant, I think I put my foot in it once again!

I was expecting the next part of my journey to be a long one but surprisingly it wasn't what I expected. On pulling up at the Red Cow Hotel stop, the driver pointed the way for me. I then noticed two Leeds fans stood at the other side of the road, realised it was the tram stop so went to speak to them about how to get to the ground. They were from Worksop and next minute someone shouted me and it was Paul just getting off a tram. It's a good job I hadn't walked straight

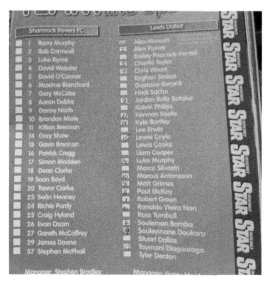

to the hotel or I would have missed him. Paul then said he would show us how to get to the ground and the tram was only a short journey there. After a short walk to the ground I couldn't believe the coincidences when I saw my friend Sue and Keith Gaunt from Fullerton Park across the road. Paul, the two lads from Worksop and I went our separate ways, the latter having now purchased their tickets thanks to Paul.

Shamrock Rovers 16.7.16

Keith said they were going to try and get into the ground to put the Fullerton Park banner up so I said I'd go with as I'd got mine with me too. What great hospitality, as a steward unlocked the gates to take us in and let us hang them up. They got pride of place behind the goal. The steward was ever so nice and this is how it should be and Shamrock should take great credit for this.

We then spent the next three hours in the Maldron Hotel opposite the ground. To begin with there was only me and those on Mick Hewitt's trip in there. Before long it was packed with Leeds fans, and to be honest I don't think they expected this and they ended up run off their feet behind the bar. I was stood at the bar and the chap said ladies first, but I don't think he was expecting my order of a latte! There was a fantastic atmosphere in there though, really happy to be back to see the Whites. Although there were many familiar faces including Rudi from Bergen, Norway with his two sons and Gerry McDermott, one of the Irish Whites, there were many I didn't know. The hotel even had a young lad playing a keyboard and singing providing the entertainment.

I went into the ground at 2.30 p.m., met up with Derek and we found Sue, who had saved us a place. By this time the sun had indeed come out and it was a very warm day, just the right thing for starting the football season off. Although as soon as I sat down I felt really tired and wanted to fall asleep! The steward who had let us into the ground earlier said that there would be mostly Leeds fans there and probably 300 home fans, and looking around that looked correct. It was great seeing all the banners behind the goal that had appeared next to ours. There were quite a few

Shamrock Rovers 16.7.16

others spotted around the ground too. There wasn't much singing, only pockets of fans, but again there was a great atmosphere around the ground. In comparison to last year in Austria, when the Frankfurt fans turned up on kick-off to cause mayhem, I much prefer no trouble!

The team for today was Green, Purver, Bartley, Bamba, Taylor, Vieira, Grimes, Botaka, Roofe, and Antonsson. Subs used were P. McKay for Bartley and Sacko for Roofe. I can't remember who went off but later there was a mass substitution with Turnbull (obviously for Green), Coyle, Diagouraga, Denton, Phillips, Murphy, Mowatt, Stokes and Doukara coming on.

As there are many new faces in our team at the moment I don't know them all, so it will take a while to get used to their names and work out who is who. It will become easier once they are given squad numbers. We also have a new manager in charge, Garry Monk. Against Shelbourne in the previous game, Leeds played with one team for 60 minutes and then swapped over with another team playing for 30 minutes. Today the latter started the game and played for 60 minutes and vice versa.

Within six minutes, though, Leeds had scored a goal when Marcus Antonsson, our new signing from Sweden, put us ahead. He also scored another after Wood scored from the penalty spot to put us three up. We hit the woodwork a few times and had a few tame shots on target that with more power behind them maybe would have scored. The only real Shamrock Rovers pressure that could have given them a goal saw Green fumble the shot but claim it at the second attempt. The game passed very quickly too, but as a start to the season in my opinion it is one of the better pre-seasons of late. Having scored some goals and played some football it is a decent start. There will be plenty of swapping the teams around over the next few games to see who will be the starting 11, and there are some promising signs that Antonsson knows where the goal is! Roofe also looks

Shamrock Rovers 16.7.16

a good prospect. I do like the Swansea link with Monk too as they got things right on and off the pitch. I realise there is a long way to go but for now, I will enjoy the fact that we won, I had a great day out and met lots of great people.

My grateful thanks go to Derek for dropping me off at the Interchange to catch my bus back to the airport. I arrived back there just after 6.00 p.m., which I knew was early for my 9.00 p.m. flight but I'd rather be there than panic, thinking I'm not going to make it in time. Not like one lad on the plane who said they'd still been in the pub at 7.30 p.m., but had made it on time to find the plane had been delayed an hour. I was there all that time and then could have missed it! I had stayed in one part of the airport and the lad I know from Sherburn was there with another lad. I started to think it was very quiet there, the boards kept saying that the plane was still delayed till 21.55 but no announcements or anything. It did give the gate number though. At 9.30 p.m. I said that if the plane was going at that time I would rather go down to the gate to check it out and they agreed, and we started walking and walking and realised that it was a long way to the gate! Around halfway there one of them said I think that was an announcement that they were boarding our plane, so we all began to run. After five minutes, though, I'd had it and told them to run on. I kept going for the easy option of the moving escalators but did manage to get there. We didn't realise there was this part of the airport but it seemed to be where most of the people were. There were other Leeds fans on the plane, plus some Newcastle who had been playing near to where the Leeds team had trained.

I eventually arrived home at 00.35 a.m., totally shattered after approximately 20 hours of travelling but still glad I'd had the opportunity to go. Put it this way, some fans have to do this every time they want to see Leeds play which is remarkable and well done to them!

My next game will be Guiseley next Friday and then the home game before the season starts for real, so see you as usual in the Peacock for the latter. LUFC – Marching on Together!

GUISELEY – 22 JULY 2016

Although Garry Monk was going to use two separate teams for the visit to Guiseley today and Peterborough tomorrow, I was still looking forward to seeing us play. I won't be going to Peterborough as I will be spending the day with my family.

I drove to Guiseley and parked up in good time before getting an ice cream and going into the ground. Although tickets were not on sale they were allowing Leeds fans to pay at the turnstiles. As I put my banner up behind the goal Stix went past and spoke to me, then I made my way to the main stand and the seats. There were already a few familiar faces in the crowd and it was good to see everyone. Just before the game was due to start I went back down the stand and saw Peter Lorimer stood next to Stix. I knew Peter had been ill, so I said hello to him and was glad to see that he recognised me straight away and asked if I was still writing, to which my answer was yes. I got a photo of him on the way back after asking him if it was alright to take one of him. It's sad to see him look a shadow of himself and good luck with his recovery.

The team was Silvestri, Coyle, P. McKay, Diagouraga, Denton, Phillips, Vieira, Botaka, Stokes, Doukara, Wood and Turnbull replaced Silvestri at half-time. The trouble is, half of them look different without their names on the back and I couldn't work out who was who for the younger ones.

As we kicked off Guiseley started off very strong, and before we knew it we were three goals down and it felt like normal service had resumed. Oh dear. With Silvestri back in goal it would be easy enough to say he was at fault but to be honest he pulled off some great saves, but if I remember correctly, Guiseley scored from the rebounds. Diagouraga was in the back four and I didn't think he looked comfortable in that position. A woman behind me said that Guiseley had been in this position before, three goals up and had lost it, so it could all change yet. I suppose she must have been psychic! We pulled one back just before the break when Stokes scored to give some hope that we wouldn't get totally hammered.

I went to tie my banner back up at half-time and then saw that we had a massive dog in the stands, although I'm not sure who it supported! I then stood talking to Dave Watkins and others before going back to my seat for the second half.

What a difference, as Leeds seemed to have come out with a purpose, although we were back to only playing half a game of football. The ball kept going from end to end but after one attack with Botaka going forward, he ended up scoring. Phillips then scored a beauty from outside the area and finished with Doukara getting the winner. Before half-time I didn't think we'd ever score one, never mind four, but it was nice to finish outright winners as Guiseley seemed to run out of steam. As it goes, Guiseley had the better of the first half and us the second half.

At the end of the game I decided to wait at the players' entrance, as I was driving and didn't need to rush off. There were lots of kids waiting with their parent(s) and it was nice to see them so excited. Garry Monk came out to be interviewed by Thom Kirwin, Katherine Hannah and others, as many of the players came out and had photos and signed autographs. Eventually someone said there was no one else left in the dressing room, as the players (from both sides I think) had sneaked out of the emergency exit. Now, to me that is very bad taste for all the kids there. I'm not bothered about myself, but one thing the players should never do is ignore the fans, because without us they would be nothing!

I'd decided to wait until Monk came off the pitch, but after his interviews were over he was in a very long conversation with someone who I later found out to be Ben Mansford, our new CEO I think. I'm sure he must have been talking to him for a good 25 minutes and there were a few fans still there when he came off the pitch and I managed to get a photo with him.

I honestly didn't think we could come back from three goals down, so it felt good to know that we had. I know many of the team who played tonight probably won't be the first 11, but the second-half performance got them out of jail.

My next game will be a week tomorrow, for our only home game of the pre-season before our opening game at QPR. I would think after the Peterborough game tomorrow Monk will have some idea of who he wants in his first 11 and the squad numbers will be issued. I would expect our main first 11 will get to play together as a team next week to give them a chance to gel. Hopefully we can get off to a good start for real. After having a stressful time of late personally, I am looking forward to having some family time tomorrow, although one of the lads at the players' entrance did offer to take my camera to Peterborough for me! See you next week, LUFC – Marching on Together!

ATALANTA – 30 JULY 2016

The last pre-season game, but our first at Elland Road, came after I set off from Guildford this morning at 8.20 a.m. After a horrendous 8½-hour journey to get there yesterday, the worry was that I wouldn't get back in time for kick-off. Luckily the traffic was kind to us and I managed to drop my daughter off at home before heading back to Elland Road.

After parking up, I took a couple of photos just as I reached the traffic lights. With that, someone turned round to me and said they had just been talking about me! It was some of the Selby LUSC lads from Hornsea who used to travel with us in the eighties; one lives in Thailand now and was over for the game. Just as I said goodbye to them, I turned round to see Ian and Keenan. It's funny that I'd just posted a photo to my Facebook page this week of a Leeds United apron I'd had since the seventies. I had to remind Ian that he'd bought it for me!

I headed into the Peacock and said hello to a number of people before I found Sue and Keith. At least I managed to have a chat before Sue went into the ground. I went to queue for a quick drink as it was getting near kick-off, and a fan from Norway wearing a Duncan pub T-shirt came to chat. I said his photo would appear on the internet tonight and had a chat about my books with him. Also had a chat and some photos with some Scarborough Whites, including one over from

Atalanta 30.7.16

Australia. As usual, great Leeds United support from all over the world!

I thought I'd end up missing kick-off as I was talking so much, surprise, surprise. Luckily my watch was a few minutes fast as I got in the ground just as the teams were coming out. I had wondered why there were so many fans still outside the ground or on the concourse below the stand not rushing to get in.

The East Stand and Kop were the only places open today, which were pretty full, plus approximately 100 Italian fans in the away area. It was lovely to hear 'Marching on Together' being belted out by everyone too and good to be back.

As it was a friendly, today would have us guessing who our starting 11 would be against QPR. The team to start was Green, Taylor, Bamba, Diagouraga, Vieira, Mowatt, Wood, Roofe, Dallas, Perico and Bartley. Subs used were Coyle for Perico and Sacko for Dallas, who came on immediately at the start of the second half. Other subs used were Grimes for Diagouraga together with Phillips for Mowatt and later Antonsson for Wood, then Murphy for Vieira and Botaka for Roofe.

It was going to take me some time to work out who was who but at least the players had their names and numbers on, although I was surprised to see Perico with both on his shirt as he was on trial for a week. I thought it was possible that with this game being the last one prior to the season starting, this meant the players had to have them? Hopefully someone can enlighten me. Although Perico hadn't set the world alight and ended up getting himself booked today, it may mean he has a memento to take away from his one and only home performance; who knows, unless he has already signed?

As I made my way to my seat, it was weird seeing so many faces I didn't know around my usual place in the Kop. Although there were a few faces that I knew, and one next to me luckily, I couldn't work out at first which was my seat, oops!

The first half had quite a few crunching tackles flying in from both sides, although one of the Italians was rolling about after one tackle. I'm sure the ref was getting ready to book our player, only for him to get up as if nothing had happened. One thing I cannot stand is seeing players cheat by pretending they are hurt as there is no need for it. All of a sudden we got the ball into the net at the South Stand end only for confusion, with us being awarded a penalty instead for a handball I believe. Wood strolled up to take the penalty and put it away to send us into the lead. It was nice to see him get the ball without the recent antics of Antenucci, who always tried to take the ball from him. Unfortunately, Atalanta equalised just before half-time with a great goal to send us in on equal terms. It was good to see some regular faces downstairs during the break and say hello to many and have a chat, before I headed back up to my seat.

I couldn't believe the amount of people sat down in the Kop though, as I can't remember the last time I did that! Although to the top left of me everyone was standing, I decided to join everyone else around me and actually sat in my seat, so that I wasn't the only one stood up!

At the start of the second half Monk had subbed both Perico and Dallas. We had a few good

Atalanta 30.7.16

moves going from defence into attack. After a further couple of subs we went into the lead from a corner from Phillips when Roofe managed to put the ball into the net from a close angle. Although we had a further goal disallowed and Atalanta also had one disallowed, there were plenty of players getting stuck in and chasing the ball if it was lost.

The Atalanta fans could be heard for quite a bit of the game, although not too loudly. It had been very quiet from our fans for the majority of the game and it was nice to finish the last 10 minutes with some singing and chanting.

The positives from the team today were seeing Green make a couple of great saves and also catch the ball at a corner! Vieira kept getting stuck in and played well. Listening to his interview on BBC Radio Leeds after the game, he said he lost the ball and they scored but it hadn't been obvious to me. Initially after a couple of hairy moments Bamba, who was captain, and Bartley started playing better together. I'm not sure if this is going to be Monk's defence partnership but I suppose it depends on Cooper getting fit. There were individual moments from a few others and it was good to get the win even though it was a 'friendly'. Not that you'd have thought it from some of the tackles though!

After the game, I met Paul at the Peacock who wanted to buy a couple of my books, and my grateful thanks go to him. After a chat I headed for home, ready to upload my photos. I then saw the *Yorkshire Post* had stolen my thunder. They had circulated a photo of the Directors' box showing Cellino sat with a couple of gentlemen which I had got too! There have been rumours circulating once again about interested parties (Chinese) buying Leeds. As usual I will wait and see if anything materialises, because as usual you can't second guess what will happen with us!

A week tomorrow sees the start of the football for real with our trip to QPR. With it being an early kick-off this means we have a very early departure time from Leeds of 5.00 a.m. At least I'll be able to sleep on the coach! I look forward to catching up with many of our fans and seeing what Garry Monk, his backroom staff and our team can produce on the pitch for us. See you there, LUFC – Marching on Together!

CHAPTER 2 – AUGUST 2016

QPR – 7 AUGUST 2016

A 3.30 a.m. get-up call beckoned for the first game of the season at QPR. Our first early kick-off due to the televising of the game by Sky was also the reason for the early start. As it was, we had a good run down to London and arrived in Uxbridge for our stop in good time. As well as the Fullerton Park Branch, there were also the Worksop and West Midlands branches that joined us there. We also had some supporters of our enemy over the Pennines turn up. Sue and I had to laugh at one Leeds lass, who went past and gave them a withering look in their direction. I think that's an automatic reaction for some reason!

We arrived at the ground an hour before kick-off and had the long walk around the ground to get to the upper tier seats. After a quick bag and flag inspection, Sue and I got into the ground and went to find somewhere to hang my flag and the Fullerton Park flag up. We did this and proceeded to our seats ready for the kick-off. The Leeds mascot was the nephew of one of our members, so I had been asked to look out for him and get some photos. About 15 minutes before kick-off I saw a steward who seemed to be looking anxiously at our flags, and I wondered if he was trying to find

QPR A 7.8.16

QPR A 7.8.16

the owners? As it turned out he was, and we were asked to move them from where we had put them. He was very helpful though and he took us to where we could hang them over the front of the stand, but unfortunately there was nowhere to tie them. With that we were able to hang them at the back of the stand.

Today was Monk's first League game in charge as manager of Leeds. The team was Green, Berardi, Taylor, Bartley, Bamba, Diagouraga, Vieira, Wood, Dallas, Grimes and Roofe. Unfortunately, Berardi was subbed by Coyle very early on with what looked like a recurrence of his recent injury. To be honest, I was surprised that he had started the game today, with not being involved in much pre-season training. Antonsson came on for Grimes and Sacko for Roofe.

I was open-minded about how we would play, because the only concerns I could say were that we had a lot of new members in the team and it would be a case of how we would play and gel against Championship opposition. As it was, it didn't take long to find out! QPR won a corner and just as they were ready to take it, the Leeds fans were screaming at the ref for the ball not being correctly placed. As the ref actually took notice and made the player roll the ball back, I said to the lad next to me that it was nice for the ref to take notice of the fans. With that, I also said I only hope they don't score from it now! A comedy show seemed to be the way with what happened next, as the ball I think hit the post and was cleared then not cleared and ended up in the back of the net to put them into the lead. With less than five minutes on the clock we had an uphill battle ahead of us. At least it would give us an indication of the character of the team to get back into the game.

QPR A 7.8.16

As it is, the first half was not a good one, as Leeds struggled to get any momentum going. I had been really disappointed in Diagouraga this pre-season as he didn't seem at all comfortable in the positions that he had played in. Immediately at the start of the game, Charlie Taylor came under stick from the chap a couple of seats away from me and I told him I disagreed. As his response was that it is his opinion, he is entitled to it, and in that sense so am I. I find it very sad that once again a player is being hung out to dry by a media campaign. In my opinion this is wrong and should be held behind closed doors, as this does not benefit the team at all. Also, Charlie Taylor and Lewie Coyle were the ones who had most of the ball in the first half and stood out for me, whereas the response was that Charlie was rubbish and should be sold for being a Judas! Sorry but I disagree. We also continued with the same formation as we have with the last few managers which have been one up front. This hasn't worked with any of them and it didn't work once again today, so why we have to continue with this is beyond me?

The second half was slightly better and things improved when Antonsson came on and we changed formation. When Sacko came on he immediately livened the game up and looking at it, he should have been on from the start. Unfortunately, a few minutes later QPR got a penalty to go further into the lead and make it even harder to come back from. We did try to get some attacking going and came close a couple of times. I don't actually think Smithies had

QPR A 7.8.16

one save to make on target, though, as our first shot in the first half was off target on about 43 minutes! To cap it all, in injury time QPR got a third goal to well and truly hammer us!

At the end of the game there were boos ringing out from many fans as the players came to clap us. I didn't boo or clap them and just went to collect my flag instead. It felt like I was resigned to our plight already!

The next couple of weeks will be very telling as to where we are going to be heading as a team. I honestly feel there will be more players going out, but will that be to the detriment of the team even more? With Cook being sold, and I was strongly against that too, I am firmly of the belief that we should have kept the spine of the team and built on it rather than replace so many at once. Obviously time will tell, but if the team puts out a performance like this next week for our first home game then we will be in big trouble. I am sure there are going to be changes to the starting 11, but first we have a visit to Fleetwood, which will be a new ground for me to visit. Monk has got a big challenge on his hands but what I will say is, although I like the appointment, I was very disappointed to see him standing on the side-line today but seemingly being very quiet during the game.

After the social media hype from many Leeds fans over the last few weeks, it is back to reality! We have a long way to go and also things can turn round very quickly. Let's hope that happens and soon and fingers crossed we head in the right direction. See you at Fleetwood – LUFC – Marching on Together!

FLEETWOOD, EFL CUP – 10 AUGUST 2016

I was pleased that the draw had given me a new ground to visit, although we had to be careful there wasn't going to be another Cup upset. It was also a game where we were up against an ex-Leeds manager in Uwe Rosler, who had been sacked early last season. I had left Halifax in glorious sunshine so had never given it a thought that it might rain. Must be because we crossed the Yorkshire border!

We arrived at the ground in good time at 6.00 p.m. and were directed immediately to Jim's bar, their club, and it was nice to be welcomed. It also reminded me of the good old days of Fullerton Park Supporters' Club, which is no more. In those days we also went in other teams' clubs before and after games, although not all were so welcoming, Man City being one! The first Leeds fans we met in there were from Sweden and it was nice that they asked for a photo with me as well as the one I took of them!

As we headed into the ground it was still raining, and it was then I noticed we had the standing terraces behind the goal as well as the seats down the side where I was. A lad was stood outside the turnstiles and he was talking about his flag, saying it had cost £90 and he wasn't going to leave it or something to that effect. As I got to the front of the stand I was talking to a couple of our stewards, who said the lad had been chucked out. They said I could go and hang my flag in the standing part, but apparently I wouldn't be allowed back in this stand. This was disappointing, as an email received by one of our branch members from Fleetwood had said they welcomed flags as long as they didn't cover any adverts up. I suppose this could have been the case!

The team today was Green, Cooper, Bartley, Taylor, Vieira, Phillips, Wood, Pablo Hernandez making his debut, Coyle, Roofe and Sacko. Subs were Bamba for Cooper, Mowatt for Sacko and Antonsson for Vieira.

After the shambles of our first League game at QPR, we were looking for a better performance all round from the team. Unfortunately, we looked to have carried on the same regardless, despite some changes in the team personnel. Within 15 minutes we were a goal down yet again and there were plenty of disgruntled fans in the stand as the tensions of being a Leeds fan rose once again. We did have a couple of tame shots on target which was an improvement on QPR! I will say that once again that lone striker up front does not work and Wood needs support.

At half-time we were joking whether or not it would be a good idea to go up for the second half! It was still raining relentlessly and you would never have guessed it was the middle of August. I put my flag across the middle of the stand underneath the Keighley Whites flag. A couple of nice stewards helped to secure it at their end of the seats. Adam Pope, Noel Whelan, Eddie Gray, Neil Redfearn and Thom Kirwin were just across from me keeping listeners entertained on the radio, which was far better than what had been on the pitch. It was nice when Peter Lorimer saw me and waved. He looks so ill at times, but it was nice to have the recognition from him.

To me the game changed when Mowatt came on for Sacko. Immediately you could see that the players around him responded better. We put some pressure on, but then when Antonsson came on and gave Wood support…well, what a difference! We actually started putting pressure on and in the final minutes of the game equalised when Antonsson stuck the ball into the net. The only downside was it meant 30 minutes of extra time, which wasn't good for those fans already soaked through! It wasn't long before we got a penalty and Wood stuck it away to put us into the lead for the first time on the night. This began to give us some hope, but in the second half of extra time Fleetwood equalised to send the tie into penalties.

For the first time in as long as I can remember, we actually put five penalties in a row into the net, with Green saving Fleetwood's fifth one to win the tie. Scoring from the spot were Wood, Antonsson, Mowatt, Phillips and Hernandez. The Leeds fans were very noisy trying to put their player off and the cheers when Green saved were brilliant, as all our pent-up emotions were released! It was great to know we had gone through on penalties for once. At the end of the game it was nice to see Alex Mowatt go across to Rosler to shake his hand, and I was told Bamba had done the same. They then went to clap the Leeds fans with the rest of the team.

As we made our way back to the coaches, we came across some lads trying to carry one of our disabled fans who had been struggling with the long walk back to the coaches. As I got to the back of the parked coaches I mentioned this to a policeman stood there, and also to Chris Beeton whose coach he was on. I also mentioned it to the police stood at the front of the coaches and they said they were aware of it and wouldn't be rushing off. That was a relief!

As the draw for the next round was taking place immediately after all the games had finished tonight, we found we had been drawn at Luton away. Luckily, I'm still off work and will be able to go to that one. Our first home game on Saturday against Birmingham promises a large crowd and I look forward to this win tonight giving us something to build from. I didn't think Pablo would last the pace but he did, and actually did okay for his first game. Charlie Taylor was also involved in a lot of our moves once again but he looked even better once Alex Mowatt came on, as to me they are on the same wavelength and played well together. Roofe also came close a few times and was prepared to take a shot and I like the look of Antonsson, especially when he scored! Although Fleetwood were a lower league team, they did put us under pressure and were able to score two goals, so Saturday will be telling in how we perform against other teams in our division. Looking forward to it so see you there LUFC – Marching on Together!

BIRMINGHAM – 13 AUGUST 2016

As Leeds were at home today, it should have been a relatively late start to go to Elland Road. Instead I left home at 3.30 a.m. and drove to Oxford and back to pick up my brother Rolf, who has broken his leg, and a big thank you to his friend for meeting me halfway. It was funny when on the M1 on our return journey; I heard a horn sounding and looked to the car in the lane to my

Birmingham 13.8.16

right to see a Leeds fan giving me the salute! Obviously that was reciprocated! After leaving Rolf in Brighouse, and returning to Leeds with my daughter Michelle and granddaughter Laura, at least the traffic was good to us. I had arranged to meet one of the lads from the old Selby Branch of the Supporters' Club who was on the committee with me. I hadn't seen Paul since I gave up running the branch in 1992, and headed to the Peacock to meet him. As I arrived in the car park this lad shouted out to me and asked if I remembered him. I hadn't seen David Scott from Selby since the seventies and he had come over for the game from South Africa! I couldn't believe the coincidence of us arriving at the pub at the same time! I had a quick word with my friends Sue and Paul and headed up to the Peacock garden.

It was good to be back and there were no end of people saying hello, including Terje from Norway. I even had a happy birthday sang to me by the Wakefield Whites, even though my birthday was a couple of days earlier! I made sure I was going into the ground in good time, as I had been asked to get some photos of Ray Fell leading the team out. Ray has recently resigned his post of Chairman of the Leeds United Supporters' Club due to ill health and this was a lovely gesture by the club. Just as I neared the Kop I heard someone shout my name, and it was Gregory Phua from Singapore over to watch the game. I had said if he saw me to shout me for a photo, and he did. Fantastic support from our worldwide fan base once again. Unfortunately, I missed seeing one of our fans from America as I didn't see a message from him on my phone until I got home.

There was a great buzz around the place and I was hoping that we could keep that, obviously it all depended on what happened during the game. The team today was Green, Bamba, Bartley, Taylor, Vieira, Sacko, Wood, Antonsson, Mowatt, Hernandez and Ayling making his debut. Subs were Roofe for Wood, Phillips for Mowatt and Dallas for Hernandez.

The opening 15 minutes saw Leeds put on a lot of pressure and play attacking football, which was good to see. It was also good seeing Alex Mowatt back in the side, as he has been missed in my opinion. Unfortunately, as is always the case, we conceded a goal seemingly against the run of play. Straight from our attack that had seen Antonsson come close to scoring, Birmingham raced to the other end in front of the Kop to slot the ball home under Green's advancing body. Although Birmingham had scored I didn't feel too downbeat, as we had been playing well with the best football seen by the team so far this season/pre-season. We equalised approximately 15 minutes later after Mowatt played a great through ball to Sacko, whose hard shot went through the goalie's hands. There had been some good signs that the players could gel as a team and I was quite positive as we went into the break on equal terms.

Unfortunately, within 10 minutes of the second half, Birmingham were attacking the South Stand when I saw the ball end up with one of their players in acres of space, right in front of the goal. There was no way he was going to miss that and he didn't. That's when my heart sank that we would have to get back into the game from a goal down once again. Although we came very close

Birmingham 13.8.16

to an own goal equaliser, things were starting to get tense on the terraces, but I'm not sure when things deteriorated on the pitch. After a good first half the second one ended up with us running out of steam. It got to the stage when we lost whatever shape we did have and there was no way we would get anything out of the game.

That is two losses out of two at the start of this season's campaign and we have a big challenge ahead of us, and Monk has got to get things going in the right direction and quick. As we have another home game on Tuesday against Fulham, we will not have long to wait to see how we will react.

As we were heading towards Billy's statue I was shouted by a friend who is going through a tough time at the moment. I had to give her a big hug just to let her know that she has the support of other Leeds fans at this time. Regardless of what does or does not happen on the pitch, this is what being a Leeds United supporter is all about, knowing we can count on others in times of need.

I half expected to want to fall asleep during the game today due to my early start, but for once I hadn't felt that way; not that it made a difference to the scoreline! After having a great crowd for our first home game of over 27,000 fans today, who had been full of high hopes, many were brought down to earth rapidly with a bang. Personally, I don't expect many things to change but on our first half performance, that had given me hope. Realistically it is going to be another hard season but it is too early to call things at the moment. I'm hopeful of Monk getting time to give us some stability on and off the pitch, but unfortunately that decision is not down to me!

See you all on Tuesday – LUFC – Marching on Together!

FULHAM – 16 AUGUST 2016

After Saturday's game where we remained pointless, it was vital that we got something out of the Fulham game tonight. I picked up an excited granddaughter Hannah and her mum, the latter who was hoping for a win for her birthday. It was another glorious day so most people were outside the Peacock, but as we didn't get there till nearly seven we stayed inside to chat. Keith Gaunt said that I should have been there earlier, as some fans from Johannesburg were in with a very large flag. I was sorry to have missed them. One of the Norwegian Whites came in, one from Belfast and then another from America. Just before we left the Peacock, Keith said I'd just missed the Singapore Leeds fans outside too! Gregory Phua has agreed to share a couple of photos from the Singapore members which I've included in mine.

As it got near kick-off we went to go in the ground, when one of the lads I knew stopped me for a chat. Hannah then had a photo taken with the lone piper who was playing outside the club shop. By doing that, it seems we missed Lucas the Kop Cat! I was surprised to see the queues outside the turnstiles at the Kop end, though, when we got there. Although the crowd was a lot lower than Saturday, I still wasn't expecting this and unfortunately missed kick-off because of it.

The team today was Green, Cooper, Ayling, Bartley, Taylor, Phillips, Wood, Antonsson, Roofe, Dallas and Hernandez. Subs were Vieira for Dallas, Mowatt for Hernandez and Sacko for Roofe.

Fulham H 16.8.16 Gregory Phua Singapore

The game started off at a fast pace and there was plenty of play from both sides. After a while it quietened down, but although at times we looked threatening, Fulham did as well. Matt Smith had returned to Elland Road once again playing for Fulham, but McCormack had been sold recently. At one point in the first half, as Fulham were attacking the Kop, they played some really nice passing football and we had a narrow escape not to go a goal down. I think the ball hit the upright where luckily we managed to clear it up-field. We did have a couple of chances, but to be honest there was a real fear that Fulham would score instead.

At half-time we couldn't find our friends so went back into the stand, and saw there was going to be some entertainment with penalties. A lad stood to the right of where we were was chosen to go onto the pitch. I didn't realise that they had to put their hand on the ball and go round 10 times before kicking the penalty. It was so funny watching him falling over once and scoring one penalty out of the three. Hannah had gone behind the goal as Lucas the Kop Cat was the goalie. After the penalties had finished, I told her to go after him to have a photo. We managed to do this in front of the West Stand, where another boy got in the photo too. It's nice to see the kids so happy when they can do this!

About five minutes into the second half some lads at the back of the Kop to our left started to get some singing going, and it was really good when we had a 10-minute spell with everyone getting behind the team. Eventually this died down but I had enjoyed the atmosphere. We did manage to get forward many times and did come close, but it was Green who was called to make a fantastic save to prevent Fulham from scoring. Eventually, though, it was Fulham who took the lead with a long-range shot and it was looking like we were going to be empty-handed once again. If it ended up this way that would certainly put a lot of pressure on Monk and the team.

When four minutes of injury time was put up, the fans started getting noisier. Hannah kept shouting 'Come on Leeds' over and over, probably driving everyone mad but she wanted them to score so kept doing it. As it was, eventually others started upping their support and with two minutes to go, Wood, with an overhead kick, scored to equalise. What a relief as the pent-up emotions of the fans were let out! Wood had obviously had some stick and put his hand behind his ear to the Kop. Whatever happens, the relief around the ground was apparent and sorely needed and this could be the turning point. We have got our first point of the season so need to build on this now. It was always going to be difficult with having over half of a new team playing together. There are some good signs but it is going to take time. For now at least, let's hope we can carry on in the right direction.

At the end of the game we bumped into Jo who stands behind us in the Kop, and she said instead of Mr Angry we now have Miss Squeaky. We went to Billy's statue for photos and found some Australian Leeds fans there and they asked if I could take a photo of them, which I did. I also met some from Galway. Hannah, like her sister last week, wanted her photo taken with the policemen, who obliged. When she said she was a lucky charm, one of them said that when it was the return game at Fulham, she wasn't allowed to go! An opposition supporter in our midst but they were a good laugh!

As we head to Hillsborough and Sheffield Wednesday for Saturday's game, the ground has not been a good one for us as of late. Luckily the early kick-off won't affect us too much as we leave Leeds at 10.30 a.m. after meeting in Billy's bar. A reminder to our fans: they do not allow us to take our flags into the ground, and last season they also wouldn't let me take a flask in either! Sorry, but that is way over the top as what harm do they do? See you there – LUFC – Marching on Together.

SHEFFIELD WEDNESDAY – 20 AUGUST 2016

Although it was an early kick-off today, we didn't have to leave Leeds until 10.30 a.m. As I left home my brother Rolf had asked what I expected today, and I said I wasn't sure as it depended who was playing. He told me positive thinking would make us win, mmm…! Just recently I would wait and see how we played before I made a decision.

We had Annette from Denmark travelling with the branch today, and Raluca from Romania was travelling with the White Rose Branch. A warm welcome to our overseas fans; this includes Terje from Norway, who I saw at the end of the game.

As we walked to the ground after getting dropped off by the coach, it was nice to get an 'enjoy the game' from a policewomen and a couple of others smiling and saying hello. I hadn't brought

Sheffield Wednesday A 20.8 .16

my flag today due to issues last year with getting them into the ground, but I did see the Keighley Whites managed to get theirs in and hung up without an issue. Just before I went through the turnstiles I had a chat with Vaughan and his son George from Halifax, and would like to wish George a very happy birthday for tomorrow!

The team today was Green, Taylor, Bartley, Cooper, Ayling, Mowatt, Wood, Antonsson, Sacko, Vieira and Bridcutt. The latter making his debut for us having signed again this week, but not a loan this time. Subs were Doukara for Antonsson, Roofe for Mowatt and Phillips for Sacko. The attendance was 29,075. One thing I thought about was that we didn't know who was going to play for us today, but that meant Sheffield Wednesday wouldn't have known either. I also hoped that by scoring the late goal against Fulham that would be the spark to change our season, giving the team confidence.

As Leeds came out without a mascot again, I wondered why? We have lots of kids who go all over watching us; Jack is one of them and has been trying to be a mascot for ages. He is also a home and away season ticket holder. As I don't know the reason why, I will ensure I try and find out how to put his name forward.

The game kicked off with a high tempo from both sides, although Wednesday were the ones who came quite close on a few occasions. Charlie Taylor raced across the box from the other side of the pitch to take the ball off the toes of one of their players and put the ball out. We did look vulnerable on a few occasions but held firm. There were lots of positive signs from Leeds, though,

SheffieldWednesday A 20.8 .16

as the game flowed from end to end and we were very lucky that the woodwork as well as Cooper denied Wednesday a goal. From a neutral fan's point of view, they wouldn't have had anything to complain about. The only thing that got us mad was the ref giving free-kicks to them for blatant dives! Now that is something that I hate with a passion!

As we have struggled to play for 90 minutes so far this season, the talk at half-time was could we keep this up? We did actually look fitter, and Wood was one who stood out for me when he was running, showing he had picked up some speed. As I said to my friend Sue later, we were probably a few weeks behind other teams with fitness due to late signings, et cetera, but it looked like we had upped the ante today. I was also introduced to Raluca by Jo and got some photos as it's great to meet our overseas fans.

The Leeds fans had been in good voice today and didn't need the help of a drum as per the Wednesday fans. They had been pretty quiet today though, but in the second half started to get behind their team. The Leeds fans decided they'd heard enough and got behind our team, and after a brilliant cross from Sacko, Antonsson was waiting at the far post to head the ball into the net to put us into the lead. Cue delirious scenes from the ecstatic Leeds supporters who have been starved of this for so long. I just knew the ball was going into the net as soon as it came to him! Next minute we were choking on the smell of a blue smoke bomb that had appeared right in front of us. Eventually one of the lads managed to get it to the front of the stand out of harm's way.

There was always a chance Wednesday would get back into the game, but Leeds were playing as a team and played really well. With a few minutes of time left the ball came across and nearly in slow motion, Wood stuck the ball into the net to put us two goals up! Fantastic and I was so happy to see the celebrating Leeds hordes! This was then the cue for the Wednesday fans to give up and walk out so their stands were nearly empty when the final whistle went. There were jubilant scenes from both the Leeds fans and the team at the end. It was great to see Antonsson and Sacko's reactions, as I bet they have never experienced the scenes they saw today. Seeing and hearing the Leeds fans must have been awesome when looking up at the stand from the pitch! It was lovely to hear the buzz amongst our fans at the end, as everyone was saying this had been long overdue. It was so nice to just think and concentrate on the football and long may it continue!

Tuesday sees us travel to Luton for the next round of the League Cup then Forest away completes three away games in a row. As my brother pointed out to me, the positive thoughts made us win, so fingers crossed this continues. See you at Luton – LUFC – Marching on Together.

LUTON, EFL CUP 2ND ROUND – 23 AUGUST 2016

As soon as the draw for the second round of the League Cup (as I prefer to call it) was made, it cast my mind back to two games against Luton that stand out for me. The first one was when we had been on the European Cup trip to Anderlecht in 1975 with Murgatroyd's coach from Harrogate. We had spent four days in Belgium and then went straight to Luton for the away game before heading home to Leeds. We were in the opposite end to where we were yesterday, when it was an open end. I can recollect that I lost my friend Sue somehow, but can remember her going in the wrong entrance and being escorted around the pitch by a policeman to our end. The other game that stands out is when Leeds fans were banned from Luton in the eighties. We got in the same end which was by now covered, although a standing terrace. Some Leeds fans from the area had got season tickets for their end and my husband Phillip and I used them to ensure we got to see the game. I thought I'd given the game away when I put the ticket in upside down, but luckily a steward helped me and I got in! I'm not sure if Luton were one of the first teams to have electronic tickets at the turnstile but I'm sure someone will put me right on that one!

It was a gorgeous day weather wise as we headed to Luton, and I always feel upbeat about going to football games when it is like this. My brother said I had to be positive about the result again when I said it depended who was playing and I would make my judgement when I was watching. What I didn't expect was the whole team to be changed! After a stop in Bedford, we went to Toddington services to meet the police escort to the game. At least all the traffic into Luton was stopped to let us through as we are very important people, and the locals were all out to look at us arriving.

Luton's ground is still part of the dark ages, with the away turnstiles being part of people's gardens and in between the houses. I actually like the fact that it is quirky despite the facilities not being particularly good. Luton themselves have ended up with financial difficulties which ended with them being deducted 30 points. They have had to fight their way back up the leagues, and despite everything I wish them well in this because, whatever happens, it is the fans who have to

Luton A EFL 23.8.16

suffer through others' misdemeanours which is wrong in my opinion. I put my banner up nearest the Luton stand and again a steward immediately asked if I needed help and tied the other side up for me. A big thank you to him.

The team today was Silvestri, Denton and Jansson making their debuts, Coyle, Bamba, Dallas, Murphy, Doukara, Roofe, Grimes and Hernandez. Subs were Phillips for Murphy, Mowatt for Hernandez and Cooper for Jansson. Attendance was 7,498 with a sell-out 1,510 from Leeds.

As I said above, the fact that the whole team had been changed was a new one as far as I'm aware, which hopefully wouldn't backfire on Monk. It is possible that some of the players have been put in the shop window prior to the transfer window closing at the end of the month. As we kicked off, though, although Luton were playing well and putting us under pressure, we were holding our own. The game was end to end for a lot of it too, and it was great when Denton scored a cracker of a goal on his debut. He played very well overall too, I'm delighted to say, as he is another young lad coming through the ranks. Jansson was making his debut at centre back alongside Bamba and was doing okay, although with one move he was shielding the ball waiting for Silvestri to come and get it and had to get rid when he didn't. I shouted, 'Don't wait for him to come as he never does!' Silvestri made amends a few minutes later, though, with a great save to prevent Luton from scoring. He also made another crucial great save in the second half. The one thing I noticed in the second half was Jansson winning loads of headers in the penalty area by clearing the ball well. That was a good thing and something we have struggled with in the past, although his 6ft 5in height may have had an impact on that!

Although when the substitutes were made we didn't seem to have any specific formation, the game did still go from end to end. Luton nearly scored in the final minutes but it was good to keep the score at 1–0 and for no extra time or penalties to be had. With us through to the next round we should find out later today who we are playing. The Leeds fans were in high spirits at the end of the game, which was good to see.

It was also great to have an atmosphere, with the Luton fans well up for making it a good one. Things did descend to lows at times with the Luton fans singing about Jimmy Savile and the Leeds fans responding with terrorists. At half-time the Leeds fans got the new Pablo Hernandez chant going which was very catchy. Pablo Hernandez, Pablo Hernandez, Pablo Hernandez he plays for United, with Dallas and Mowatt. I may have missed something off that as I couldn't work out the middle parts as my hearing wasn't very good.

We had a police escort away from the ground and were back on the motorway very quickly. Apart from roadworks causing tailbacks we arrived back in Leeds at 1.15 a.m., which was good. Unfortunately for me, I got all the way to Halifax when I was turned back by police by Shibden Park due to an incident. The road was closed into Halifax and would be for at least another 30 minutes, so I had to do a detour by Ploughcroft to get home. I couldn't understand why the road hadn't been closed at Hipperholme giving us a different option, as the other road wasn't the best to go on. Luckily for me, I was still off work, so for once the 2.00 a.m. return home wasn't an issue for me as I wasn't picking my granddaughters up until the afternoon. Obviously some of our fans won't have been so lucky, having to be in work. I actually enjoyed our visit to Kenilworth Road despite the ground being stuck in the dark ages, because it still had that old-fashioned atmosphere about it.

We have now got Forest away on Saturday and can hopefully build on our win at Sheffield Wednesday last week. Monk seems to have got good vibes going between the squad, and I am hopeful that things are heading in the right direction on the pitch.

One last thing, a Leeds fan who sadly lost his baby son last week who was born prematurely has asked whether I could add his fundraising charity link into my blog, which I am happy to do. After losing my baby daughter Charlotte at seventeen days old, I know the pain the family are going through. Young Tommy died at six days old and his dad has got a home shirt with his name and the number six on his back in memory of his son. The link is https://www.justgiving.com/fundraising/tommysbattle and they are raising funds for Sands, the stillbirth and neonatal death charity because people need support through loss of children. If anyone feels they could contribute then your donations would be very welcome.

See you all at Forest, LUFC – Marching on Together!

NOTTINGHAM FOREST – 27 AUGUST 2016

After a very bad night's sleep once again, when my alarm went off I could have turned over and slept for a week. My incentive of going to follow Leeds, though, made me get up and head to

Billy's bar for the coach. After stopping in Mansfield, we arrived at the ground half an hour before kick-off. Luckily we avoided the rain and were in the stands when it started.

At the Sheffield Wednesday game, I wrote about the lack of a mascot at the game. I had been speaking to one of our fans about it as his son would have done it. I'm pleased to say that Jack had got his wish and was to be our mascot today at Forest. As I was looking for my seat someone tapped me on the shoulder, and as I turned round, planted a kiss smack on my lips. As someone else pointed out, it was the drink they insisted that did it lol!

The team today was Green, Bartley, Cooper, Taylor, Ayling, Bridcutt, Antonsson, Sacko, Vieira, Wood and Hernandez. Subs used were Phillips for Vieira, Roofe for Sacko and Mowatt for Hernandez. Attendance was 20,995 with 1,925 Leeds fans.

Although Monk had changed the whole team for the midweek Luton Town game, I hoped that the team who won at Sheffield Wednesday last week would be maintained. As it was, the only change was Hernandez for Mowatt. The game kicked off and although things were quite even in that we had a lot of possession, we didn't put pressure on their goalie. This means also that we have to take any chances that come our way, especially if they are hard to come by. Leeds had just defended a corner very well and at that time I didn't feel that we would succumb very easily. As usual, though, I shouldn't have opened my mouth, because when Forest won their next corner the ball came into the middle and missed everyone but their player at the far side of the goal, who hoisted the ball above everyone into the net. I had looked at the team we had out and to be honest

Nottingham Forest 27.8.16

Nottingham Forest 27.8.16

they looked capable enough on paper, but as with everything they had to learn to play as a team. Hernandez got the ball a lot but many passes were wayward. He did manage a few good through balls, though, but we didn't manage to do too much with them. Taylor got the ball a lot and put many crosses in but we didn't have any clear-cut chances really.

In the second half, no changes were made by Monk as the referee started to pull us up for anything and everything. We won some 50:50 balls and were still pulled up for it. At this moment in time I started to worry that Vieira, who had already been booked, would be sent off. Although I didn't think there had been anything wrong with his tackles and he'd played well, I was hoping that Monk would see this and sub him, which he did. Phillips came on in his place and also played well. When I saw Roofe coming on, I knew that Sacko would be taken off, and unfortunately within a minute Forest scored a second goal, again from a corner. With that I felt that there was no way back. It wasn't until Mowatt came on for Hernandez, a substitution that I felt should have been made sooner, that a little bit of hope was felt. We won a free-kick and Phillips curled a fantastic free-kick straight into the net to pull one back. I really hoped that we could get something out of the game despite not really deserving it. Even though there should have been more than five minutes injury time due to a Forest player being down, subs and time-wasting, it wasn't a surprise that we only played for the five. Unfortunately, again it was Forest who got their third goal to put the game beyond us.

Looking back, I don't feel that Green is tall enough in goal. The fact that Jansson is 6ft 5in and at Luton, when he made his debut, was able to head loads of balls out of the area, we should be looking to start him next time. As Cooper went down injured again I only hope he isn't still carrying an injury after being brought back too soon. I don't think this was one of the worst displays I have seen from a Leeds team, although for some reason we never looked like scoring. It is still very early days with Monk at the helm and it doesn't look like he has found his starting 11 as yet. Personally, I would have started with the same team who won at Wednesday, but whether that would have made a difference who knows.

To cap the bad day off, on the way home on the motorway our coach pulled on to the hard shoulder when the water belt broke. I wasn't looking forward to staying on the coach until it got mended, but luckily for us another JB coach pulled onto the hard shoulder in front of us and took 30 of us back to Leeds on it. The others had to wait for either a relief coach or for it to be mended, but were approximately an hour or so behind us. It was atrocious weather on the way back with the rain and spray, but luckily going back to Halifax it wasn't as bad so maybe it had missed us.

Our support today shows to me how far and wide they come from. There were still lots of familiar faces but again lots of faces that I hadn't seen before, as our supporters pick and choose their games. I'd heard some of the Norwegian fans were there and also spoke to one of our Irish fans at half-time. It was so nice to get some positive feedback about my blogs/match reports from the latter as he said he looks forward to seeing them as he cannot get to all the games. Thank you for this, as it makes me feel good! It's a shame we couldn't have continued with the atmosphere from Kenilworth Road but I suppose there wasn't a lot to shout about today, sadly. At the end of the game it was nice to see some of our young supporters who are always up for photos.

Next week sees us have a free Saturday due to the international break, something I wish was binned. Instead of having a free Saturday I would prefer playing our long-distance midweek games and getting them out of the way. Even if we had just got a momentum going as a team, all this break does, in my opinion, is put things back so you have to start again. Our next game will be Huddersfield at home on 10 September. As they have got off to a good start this season, hopefully we can upset the apple cart and beat them. Only time will tell, of course, so see you then, LUFC – Marching on Together!

CHAPTER 3 – SEPTEMBER 2016

HUDDERSFIELD TOWN – 10 SEPTEMBER 2016

The day got off to a bad start for me when my foot slipped off the garden step and I ended up on my bum at the bottom, but not before smacking my back into the step. Once I realised I was okay I got up and thought I'd got off relatively light, until I saw my hand was bleeding and later found a graze all down my arm! Oh dear. All I was bothered about, though, was that my Leeds shirt was in one piece!

When we parked up at Elland Road, with my daughter Dani and granddaughter Laura we headed up to Holbeck Moor Park, where we were going to join Martin Hywood in the final mile walk of his fundraiser for Muscular Dystrophy. As we walked through the tunnel at the edge of the park, it brought back memories from the seventies of thousands of Leeds fans walking back to the station. Those were the days!

When we arrived at Elland Road it was fantastic to see the Leeds fans stood around clapping en masse for Martin's achievement, which was no mean feat. A big well done to him and also to everyone else who turned out to walk with him.

As I walked alongside the South Stand, I met some Leeds fans from Norway who I had met on our pre-season tour over there last year. That seems so long ago now! As the weather had turned out okay, which I hadn't been expecting, there was a big crowd in and out at the Peacock. Those

Huddersfield H 10.9.16

Huddersfield H 10.9.16

inside watching the football, whilst those in the garden listened to a band. Thanks to all those who took time to ask me how I was after my little accident this morning, which was appreciated.

As we were walking to the Kop we took the opportunity of having our bags checked on the way round, to save time at the turnstiles! There was going to be a big crowd today as Huddersfield were top of the League, so for once had sold out all their tickets. With many of our fans picking and choosing games, this was one that they had decided to come to.

The team today was Green, Jansson making his home debut, Bartley, Ayling, Sacko, Mowatt, Taylor, Phillips, Wood, Bridcutt and Antonsson. Subs were Roofe for Sacko and Doukara for Antonsson. Attendance was 28,514 with 2,721 Huddersfield. I'm not sure if they did sell out?

With Huddersfield flying high at the top of the table whilst we were near the bottom, it was going to be a tough test today. Whilst feeling indifferent about the game yesterday at what to expect, as usual my hopes had built up on the way to the game. There was a good atmosphere at the start of the game although it quietened down quite a bit later on. Looking at the team on paper, it looked okay, but again with bringing 11 new players in, things are going to take time if they are going to work. We started off with the players chasing after the ball and backing each other up, which was a good sign. At one point, Jansson won the ball and as the Kop cheered, he turned to us encouraging us to do more! Whilst Huddersfield had a couple of chances (one of which I'm glad their player didn't play to the whistle), both teams had lots of possession without really doing much. The play was from end to end, though. The longer the game went on, the more I thought it looked like a game that would end in a draw, because neither side looked too dangerous. When Antonsson was brought down in the area the ref waved away claims for a penalty. I think it was the way that he landed that made it look as if he'd dived, but contact was indeed made. I didn't feel unduly worried when we went into the break on equal terms.

Unfortunately for us, though, once again it seems that we ran out of steam and couldn't really get going in the second half. Where did it go wrong? A long-range cracker scored by Huddersfield changed the game and once they were in the lead there was no going back. To be honest, I said they'd either get another one to kill the game or we'd sneak a goal and get a draw. But it was Huddersfield who nearly sneaked one with another long-range effort that had Green scrambling back to tip it over the bar. The nearest we came to equalising was in the last few minutes of injury time (eight minutes in all). Our player was in space and his header was quite tame but their goalie had to stretch to save it. If only he could have buried it? Monk himself was coming in for some stick from fans, because he was stood on the sidelines with his hands in his pockets. He doesn't seem to be geeing his players up or guiding them with tactics. The only time he showed some passion was when Huddersfield were wasting time, which they did a lot, and he waved his arms about. I do want to see him do well but he seems to be a dead man walking at the moment.

There were quite a few stoppages during the game, plus with all the substitutes and time-wasting from Town we expected at least six minutes injury time, but got two more on top. That

Huddersfield H 10.9.16

still couldn't get us that equaliser though, and Town were the ones who stayed top of the League with three points whilst we dropped into the bottom three. The longer we stay down near the bottom of the table, the harder it will be to get out. My thoughts have always been that we should have built on our players that we should have kept, instead of cashing in and having to start again with a new team and manager. With the team getting booed loudly from all the stands at the end of the game they are up against it with the crowd, who have got sick and tired of seeing the poor performances from a Leeds team. I didn't boo but I didn't clap them either. Where do we go from here? It is hard to know at this moment in time. We have Blackburn at home on Tuesday with Cardiff away and an early start next Saturday. Will we be able to get anything from them at all? Who knows, and whilst I will be at them both I would say Tuesday night's game will be a low attendance, as most night games are these days.

After Monk's interview after the game with Adam Pope for BBC Radio Leeds today, he hasn't impressed many fans at all with the way he reacted. Although I haven't heard it all, I did hear him say that he wasn't going to answer a specific question. He is definitely rattled, which isn't good at this early stage of the season, so I am hoping at least that him and the team can pick themselves up for Tuesday. Next week's game and result will be telling on where our season will head, although at the moment it is not looking good. See you on Tuesday – LUFC – Marching on Together!

BLACKBURN – 13 SEPTEMBER 2016

As we approached Elland Road, it was with much trepidation on my part. After losing to Huddersfield on Saturday and slipping into the bottom three, it was essential that we got the three points tonight. It is so easy to get sucked into a relegation battle, which meant it was vital that this did not happen. As I was expecting a low crowd tonight I also hoped this meant we would win, well that's my theory anyway! It seemed very quiet on the streets and most people were out in the garden at the Peacock and not inside. At least we got served pretty quickly! It was nice to see that some of our Norwegian fans were still here and going home the following day, which was another reason to hope we would win for them.

As we came out of the Peacock at 7.30 p.m. I couldn't believe how dark it was and the clouds looming overhead were ominous. Thunderstorms had been forecast, but as long as they kept off till I was in the ground, that was all that mattered.

The team today was Green, Taylor, Bartley, Jansson, Antonsson, Ayling, Bridcutt, Dallas, O'Kane making his debut, Hernandez and Sacko. Subs were Phillips for Bridcutt who went off injured, Wood for Antonsson and Mowatt for O'Kane. Attendance was 19,009 with 327 Blackburn fans.

The first half started more or less the same as on Saturday and I don't think there was much to shout about. It was more interesting watching the weather, as 'biblical rain' and sheet lightning was lighting up the sky above the South Stand. As the heavens opened, the majority of fans at the front of the East Stand scurried further up the stand to get away from the rain. I couldn't blame them, but felt quite sorry for our disabled fans who had to stay where they were and used waterproofs to protect themselves. It was funny when the whole Kop went 'ooh' at the same time, when fork lightning and a mighty crack of thunder had me thanking the fact that I was way back in the stand. We had heard that the Etihad had flooded for Man City's game and then postponed, so I was half expecting the same to happen here. As it turned out, our pitch stood up to things very well, which was good to see. Although both teams had a lot of possession without doing too much, we at least had a couple of tame shots on target. The positives are that they were indeed on target although they wouldn't have tested their goalie. As half-time approached, that familiar feeling that I couldn't wait for the whistle to blow came. As it turned out we had another five minutes to endure for injury time. Green had ended up clattering one of their players outside the penalty area and ended up with a head injury, which was bandaged for the rest of the game.

The second half started much the same way, and when Bridcutt went down injured again I knew he would go off. It's ironic that we have waited so long for him to come to Leeds only for him to get injured. Hopefully it won't keep him out for long. Phillips came on to replace him and then on the hour mark Wood came on to replace Antonsson. I looked at the clock and that was when the turn round occurred. Whether we changed formation or not, I couldn't be sure, but all of a sudden we stepped up a gear. Sacko was the one who made the goal when he ran at their defender and ended up past him on the bye line. Wood, who was waiting in the middle, had the easiest of tasks to put the ball into the net from close range to put us into the lead. What a relief to score a goal, as it felt like we'd forgotten how to do it! One of the Blackburn players went down injured for a while, which took the momentum out of our game. As it was, Blackburn ended up equalising with a more or less identical goal that Huddersfield scored against us on Saturday. Their player let fly from just outside the edge of the box and it was a goal all the way. Damn! Did this mean a draw would be on the cards? It nearly was a loss instead, as Green made a double spectacular save to stop Blackburn from taking the lead. Mowatt came on to replace O'Kane who'd had a steady debut. Leeds won a free-kick to the left of us and Mowatt went to take it. As we shouted for a delivery to beat the first man, Mowatt sent a sweetly placed free-kick that landed perfectly for Bartley to head the ball into the net and Leeds into the lead! Celebrations were seen all around Elland Road as the pent-up relief escaped to take the pressure off us. The game wasn't over just yet, though, as there were another seven minutes of injury time to endure, which I think turned into nine minutes! I'm also not sure what happened at the far goal but a couple of our players started pushing Sacko around for something? I thought at first they were arguing about the defending and thought they may lose it, but luckily it stopped as soon as it had begun.

We may have only really played for 30 minutes, but as I'd said to someone before the game, three points is all that matters and I don't care how we get them! We have now got to go to the early game at Cardiff on Saturday, and I wonder if we can carry on in the same vein as we finished tonight? To really pull in the right direction we need as many points as possible before anyone can really relax, so fingers crossed. See you there – LUFC – Marching on Together!

CARDIFF – 17 SEPTEMBER 2016

The things I do to follow my club Leeds United! You could say that I'd lost it well and truly when I was sat at Elland Road in my car just after 4 a.m., waiting for the coach to Cardiff that wasn't leaving until 6 a.m.! There was actually a method in my madness, as I'd been a good mum dropping my daughter off for her coach that left at 4 a.m. Normally there is only an hour difference with our set-off times, but not today. I set my alarm on my phone just in case I fell asleep, as the last thing I wanted was to miss the coach despite being there two hours early. At least I will be able to sleep on the coach. The only good thing about the early set-off for the noon kick-off is that we will be home at a decent time, or so I thought.

The trip down to Cardiff did pass quickly, due to the fact that I slept most of the way, only waking up just before Monmouth where we were due to stop for our pre-game drink. When we got to the pub we found both the Mexborough Branch (who I later found out had travelled with the White Rose Branch) and West Midlands already there. My daughter Danielle sent a picture to be included in my blog of a stalwart lone Welsh fan campaigning for Welsh independence, who they had met in the pub they were in.

Cardiff A 17.9.16

We didn't have as long a stop as usual, and got to the ground approximately 20 minutes before kick-off. As we got into the ground there was a great atmosphere below the stands, which I looked forward to carrying on in the seats. I put my banner up at the front of the stand then went and stood further up for the first half.

The team today was Green, Bartley, Taylor, Jansson, Ayling, O'Kane, Wood, Dallas, Sacko, Vieira and Hernandez. Subs were Roofe for Dallas, Antonsson for Wood and Phillips for Hernandez. Attendance was 16,608 with approximately 2,000 Leeds fans. To be honest, there didn't even look that many in the ground as the Cardiff stands were scarcely populated. The one thing I did notice (although this may have been done when we were last here) was the changing of their seat colour back to blue. I was sure the whole ground had been red at one time which had been their owner's choice. Eventually, after an uproar if my memory serves me correctly, they reverted back to their original colour. Someone will no doubt put me right on this.

The one thing about this new ground, though, is the lack of intimidation which Ninian Park had, although that's a good thing. My first ever visit there was 26 February 1972 when we played Cardiff in the FA Cup 5th round and won 2–0, with Giles scoring both goals. Personally, I didn't see any trouble as we stood near the right-hand corner of the pitch, but heard about plenty of our fans and coaches that did.

Cardiff came at us from the off and it seemed like we were under the cosh for a lot of the first half. At one point, though, Wood was through on goal, but hit the ball straight at the goalie. At least it was a chance and on target. Knowing you have to take your chances in this league I hoped it wouldn't prove costly. I would have liked to have seen Antonsson with that chance, having seen videos of him managing to beat a keeper when one on one I wondered if he could have put it away. The first half also saw some atrocious refereeing decisions once again. Seeing two of ours booked but Cardiff only get spoken to, along with some mystifying decisions, had the crowd singing 'you don't know what you're doing' and 'you're not fit to referee'. Something I agreed with entirely! Although there wasn't too much to shout about, I don't think the way we played was as bad as the last couple of games and I wasn't willing the half-time whistle to blow.

At half-time I got a rendition of 'We love you Heidi' from the South Kirkby branch whilst having their photo taken. It's nice to be appreciated! Another Leeds fan caught up with me, who I had met in Norway with her husband. Thank you for the feedback for my blog and the fact you love my photos taken of random Leeds fans!

At the start of the second half I went and stood down at the front with Vaughan and his son George who are from Halifax too, and young Jack. George was the lucky boy to get Sacko's shirt at the end of the game when he threw it into the crowd, well done George! When the 60th minute approached I said that we would start playing now, which was the same timing as against Blackburn. It turned out that I was right because a few minutes later, when we took a corner, the whistle blew which we thought was a free-kick to Cardiff. I then noticed Jansson on the floor and the Leeds fans were celebrating the fact that the referee had done the first good thing of the day by awarding us a penalty. Wood stepped forward to take it and put it into the bottom right-hand corner before coming with the rest of the team right in front of us to celebrate. It was a great feeling to be in the lead. It was also great to learn that this won me the golden goal on the coach too!

We seemed to step up a gear and we crowned the day off with a cracking goal from Hernandez, to put the game beyond the reach of Cardiff and guarantee us a win. The only disappointment was Hernandez running to the opposite side of the ground to celebrate instead of coming to the Leeds fans. Maybe it was something he did in his Swansea days, but hopefully he will learn! It was a great feeling to win away from home and also with it being live on Sky. It hadn't been a fantastic game but we were playing more as a team. Green also made a couple of great saves to deny Cardiff a goal. I don't think he is tall enough, but now with him having Jansson in front of him with his height, that has made a difference in my opinion. With him and Bartley starting to gain an understanding hopefully our defensive lapses will start to become more of a distant memory rather than a regular occurrence. I know it is still early days, but I felt today the three points were a must and am glad we got them. There was a great atmosphere back at the coaches, with a minibus having 'Marching on Together' blaring out and the fans joining in. No one wanted to leave in a hurry and it was good to see everyone so happy. When someone said we had gone up to 15th I said good, until my friend Sue pointed out the rest hadn't played yet! Silly me, I'd forgotten about our early kick-off.

Cardiff A 17.9.16

Our return journey was uneventful apart from a coach load of Burnley fans arriving at the services just after we had arrived and at the same time as the Vine Branch, resulting in some playful banter. Luckily for me I slept a lot of the way back too. Danielle's coach wasn't as lucky, as an ambulance had to be called for one of the lads who was taken ill. Fingers crossed he is okay as they remained on the hard shoulder until he was taken to hospital. I eventually arrived home at 10.00 p.m., which wasn't as early as I expected. A long day since getting up at 2.45 a.m.!

Tuesday evening sees the return of Blackburn to Elland Road for the next round of the EFL League Cup. Let's see whether we can progress to the next round, then we are back to the League on Saturday when we are at home to Ipswich. It's a good feeling to get a win especially away from home, and it has been missing for so long. Let's hope we have more to come and get back to seeing the Leeds United we want to see.

See you Tuesday – LUFC – Marching on Together!

BLACKBURN, EFL CUP 3RD ROUND – 20 SEPTEMBER 2016

I headed to Elland Road to see us play Blackburn for the second time in a week, only this time it was a Cup game. After beating them last week in the League and Cardiff on Saturday, it was a case of seeing whether we could carry on the run. It was very quiet as I got near the Peacock and

I knew it would be an even lower crowd than usual. I had originally thought it would be under 10,000, but after hearing we'd only sold 3,000 as of last Thursday, I guessed at 6,500. As it was, the official attendance was 8,488 with 463 Blackburn, so it was much better than I thought. Even though it was our lowest attendance since 1988 apparently, these are my reasons for it: our results have only picked up in the last couple of games, having played quite poorly prior to this, so people are picking and choosing their games; our fans come from all over the country and the world so not everyone can get to all the games; the prices, although good for season ticket holders, were still quite expensive plus anyone who bought on the day had a £5 surcharge. The latter is something which I don't agree with, as I feel it is not encouraging people to come. Also shutting the South Stand could have impacted on the attendance as many people like their own seats. I do feel that by engaging better with the fans things can improve, so time will tell on that score. When I got into my usual seat on the Kop, there were so many strange faces around that it felt weird. After a while I did start seeing quite a few regular Kop faces, though.

The team today had seven changes to the one that beat Cardiff on Saturday. Silvestri, Coyle, Bartley, Taylor, Cooper, O'Kane, Vieira, Roofe, Phillips, Mowatt and Antonsson. Subs were Hernandez for Vieira who went off injured, Wood for Antonsson and Mowatt for Grimes.

The game started off with their goalie making a great save from Coyle in the opening minutes. This opening pace didn't last too long, though, and it was fairly even with both teams having plenty of possession. There wasn't too much goal action, though, although Silvestri made a great save to deny Blackburn just before half-time. My initial thought on Silvestri was that his goal-kicking had improved, right down the middle of the pitch and whoever has been training him had done a good job. As soon as I said it though, the next few kicks he reverted to his usual aiming for the touchline and putting the ball straight out! When he eventually went back to the middle he got a cheer from the crowd! Initially it looked like the teams were playing for a draw, but going to extra time and penalties was not appealing and I said it had to be sorted in 90 minutes! There were plenty of passes going astray but plenty that were reaching their target. 0–0 at half-time though meant it was still even-stevens on the night.

At half-time, I was watching on the TV the penalties taken by a lad from the crowd. Even though he was looking very dizzy after going around one ball 10 times, he managed to score three times from the penalty spot and well done to him. It was actually good to see! The second half carried on from the first with not too much happening, although Silvestri again made a couple of good saves to keep Blackburn out. As it got to the 60-minute mark, once again I said we'd start playing now, but it wasn't until the 67-minute mark that things changed for the better. As it was, when Hernandez came on (58 minutes) things started to get slightly better and as soon as Wood came on I said that he would score. He was certainly up for it and he did indeed put the ball into the net on 72 minutes, after some great play down the left-hand side from Hernandez, who nearly scored. Wood mishit his first shot but it rebounded to him and he headed home, much to the

Blackburn 20.9.16 H EFL Cup

delight of all the Leeds fans. The atmosphere had been pretty quiet on the night, which is more the pity, but I think we were all relieved in the end that we saw the game out to win 1–0.

I am being selfish here now, because I want a big away tie that will be televised on the Wednesday. My daughter has her final performance at ACM, Guildford on the Tuesday night which has priority for me, so I would have to miss a home game if that was the chosen day. Whatever happens, we have progressed to the next round and the last 16. This is a way of getting into Europe too and I would love to see us carry on in this Cup, and we will know our next opponents later tonight.

Back to League action on Saturday with the visit of Ipswich, and hopefully we will stick with the team who won at Cardiff. Although O'Kane got a knock last night, hopefully it is nothing too serious. It looked like both O'Kane and Hernandez have started to find their feet which is good to see. Although we have to start playing for more than 30 minutes in a game, there is progress to be seen and it is something that will take time. Another three points on Saturday will go a long way to allaying fears of getting sucked into a relegation battle, so fingers crossed we are heading in the right direction. The more points we get, the better it will be, as it takes the pressure off the players, which should enable them to play better. That's my theory anyway! See you Saturday – LUFC – Marching on Together!

IPSWICH TOWN – 24 SEPTEMBER 2016

Before I start my blog today, I am going to skip to the end of the game. I can't remember the last time that I have been so engrossed in a game. The atmosphere was the best we have had at a home game for as long as I can remember, together with seeing the away side wilting and looking intimidated. Lastly, but not least, seeing the team perform as a team, backing each other up, having chances to score, putting the effort in and being unlucky not to have scored more! It really felt like the sleeping giant was stirring and long may it continue! Interesting that I wrote the next paragraph before the game, so I'll leave it as it is!

Before I set off for Elland Road I had a couple of jobs to do. As usual I was wearing one of my Leeds shirts, and I still maintain that it is one of the reasons that people feel comfortable to come up to me to talk about them. Some people walking their dog came up to me to ask who we were playing and if I was going to the game. At the tip, I got help with my rubbish, then had another conversation about Leeds, including Monk. I agreed he needed time for us to have some stability and move forwards. These are by no means isolated incidents; because I wear my Leeds shirts whenever I'm not at work, the amount of people who come to talk to me, including strangers, is phenomenal. We are a sleeping giant in my opinion! After picking my granddaughter up we got to

Ipswich H 24.9.16

Elland Road in good time, as I'd been asked to take some photos of someone in the Peacock. With the weather being warm and fine, the garden had many fans taking in the music from the band. There was a good atmosphere about the place too. After meeting the girls who were modelling T-shirts saying 'NEVER UNDERESTIMATE A WOMAN WHO SUPPORTS LEEDS UNITED' and getting the photos asked of me, we headed into the ground.

There looked to be a decent crowd too, and Ipswich fans filled the top part of their stand and brought more than Blackburn had. The team today was Green, Taylor, Bartley, Ayling, Jansson, O'Kane, Hernandez, Dallas, Wood, Phillips and Sacko. Subs used were Roofe for Sacko, Mowatt for Hernandez and Grimes for Dallas. Attendance was 22,554 with 902 Ipswich.

The game started with Leeds on the attack and I still can't believe how a fantastic strike from Chris Wood from the left-hand side of the pitch didn't end up in the net. I was convinced looking at it from the Kop that it had gone into the top right-hand corner of the goal! Unfortunately, it hit the post and came back out. The fans were getting behind the team, but the play kept getting held up for the ref giving free-kick after free-kick to Ipswich. It looked like a lot of cheating going on, because they were going down like flies and there weren't any really bad challenges being done. It did slow the game down for a while but although Ipswich had some corners, it was good to see that we were able to clear the ball and prevent them from scoring. They also had a deflected shot which

Ipswich H 24.9.16

Ipswich H 24.9.16

looked perilously close to going in that I was glad to see went past the outside of the post. Chris Wood looked to be on fire and was chasing after the ball, and I would say this was probably the best I've seen him play. After the half hour mark, Leeds were on the attack and Charlie Taylor put in a great cross into the middle which landed perfectly for Chris Wood to head the ball into the net for his seventh goal of the season. Cue celebrations all around and it was kept that way until half-time.

The second half saw some of the best football we have seen for some time, with Leeds dominating the play and looking like they would add to the scoreline. Sacko had a fantastic run along the left and should have scored, but unfortunately put the ball wide. The good thing was that at least we were getting into positions to look like scoring! When was the last time that we had done this for a lot of the game? To be honest, because of how we were dominating the game at the time I wouldn't have brought any subs on, this was what others around me thought too. We had got to the 70-minute mark before I realised that we hadn't brought any of the subs on and the first one ended up on 76 minutes, when Roofe came on for Sacko. Whatever happens, Sacko should be proud of his achievement today, because I can't remember the last time that anyone has had a standing ovation when being subbed. He will be a great prospect for the future I'm sure!

The three subs coming on did make a difference to the pace of the game, as Ipswich came at us a bit. The one thing we wanted was to hold on to the lead and get the three points. After some more time-wasting from the Ipswich players it was good to see only three minutes of injury time was to be played. With the amount of times Ipswich players went down, I thought we were heading for the same as the last League game of seven minutes, which thank goodness didn't happen.

At the end of the game the team received their applause, which was well deserved, and it was good to see things finally looking up and as if they are heading in the right direction. The scenes seen at Leeds today have been missing for so long and it was good to see them back again, even for a little while. Just think, how good things would be if these carry on in the same way? Fingers crossed from me, because I loved everything about it today as it reminded me of the Leeds United of old, along with the togetherness of the fans and the team. Long may it continue!

As long as we aren't brought down to earth with a bang, I'm hoping that the midweek game at Bristol City on Tuesday will go our way. I'm not being greedy, honestly! As long as we try like today, then anything can happen. If the opposition know that we are getting harder to beat and will not be a pushover, then that will be a good start! Putting the fear back into the opposition will go a long way to us heading in the right direction! See you at Bristol – LUFC – Marching on Together!

BRISTOL CITY – 27 SEPTEMBER 2016

I couldn't go with the Fullerton Park Supporters to Bristol, my usual travel to away games, as they were sharing a coach with the South Kirkby Branch and left Leeds at 9.30 a.m. I am very grateful to some more Leeds supporters who gave me the opportunity to get to the game and my thanks go to them. You know who you are! Although the game was being beamed back to Elland Road, I would much rather be at the game in person.

Luckily, we arrived in time for kick-off and I did my good deed of the day when I saw one of our disabled fans walking to the ground. I stayed with him to ensure he got in to the ground safely and to a seat at the front of the stand. I saw my friend Sue and her husband Paul, and then went and hung my banner up at the back of the stand.

The team today was unchanged from Saturday with Green, Bartley, Jansson, Taylor, Ayling, O'Kane, Dallas, Sacko, Wood, Phillips and Hernandez. Subs were Cooper for Jansson and Roofe for Dallas. Attendance was 19,699 with 2,065 Leeds fans. A great attendance from the Leeds fans on a Tuesday evening!

Hopes were high that we could get something from this game, but it wouldn't be easy. It was nice to see that Bristol now had a stand to the right of us. They had made a good job of it and it made a difference to how the ground looked instead of nothing being there.

As the game kicked off, Leeds looked as if they wanted to carry on with their winning streak. We were also seeing plenty of the ball but kept giving it away. Once again, though, we had a referee out to make a name for himself as every decision was going Bristol's way. The nearest we came to scoring in the first half was from Sacko, but the team were trying which was good to see. The Leeds fans were also in good voice and it was nice to be in a stand with good acoustics. Fantastic support once again, and even though there were plenty of our southern-based fans, plenty had travelled

Bristol A 27.9.16

down from Leeds for the game. Bristol should have had a man sent off and I was convinced I saw a blatant stamp on our player, but everyone said it was a head butt! Whether there were two things or not he should have walked, but he only ended up with a booking. Dallas also ended up in the book at the same time but what for I've no idea and everyone else was mystified too. The ref didn't even talk to his linesman, but ended up with a load of abuse from the Leeds fans for his dreadful refereeing decisions. Bristol had a couple of great chances but luckily for us they were way off target with their shots.

We had managed to contain Bristol for most of the game, but then more or less committed suicide five minutes from half-time and handed the impetus to Bristol. I'm not sure what happened in the left corner of the pitch to us, but Jansson all of a sudden kicked the ball out of the ground high up into the sky. Whether we needed a new ball or not was anybody's guess, but he ended up booked for his misdemeanour and Bristol came at us all guns blazing. It didn't end there, though, as when Bartley tried to calm him down he was still going berserk. The way Jansson reacted actually reminded me of Bamba at Derby when I thought Bamba was going to get himself sent off. Neither of them would be any good for us sent back to the dressing room. Now, I like Jansson, but he really needed to cool it as being down to 10 men would immediately put the pressure on to us. We had more or less managed to contain Bristol in the first half, and indeed looked the better team before Jansson gave them the impetus. It was a relief to go into the half-time break on equal terms, but just before we did Jansson made a tackle and then held the back of his leg. Our immediate thoughts were that he had injured his hamstring. I met a Leeds fan who enjoyed reading my blogs, every one of them, so thank you to him! I also met Vaughan from Halifax who did his 20 press ups, which he is doing at every away game to raise awareness for post-traumatic stress disorder for our service personnel and well done to him. Every time I switched my camera off there was someone else shouting my name so they had their photos taken. I don't mind really, as I enjoy taking the photos and it's good that fans want them done!

At the start of the second half Leeds were attacking our end, and it wasn't a surprise to see Jansson not come out due to his injury, with Cooper coming on in his place. We had a lot of possession but apart from silly balls giving the ball away, the one thing that didn't help was not being able to beat the first man when crossing a ball. The ref then surpassed himself by letting play carry on rather than give a free-kick to us for a foul on Hernandez! This ended up with Bristol scoring what turned out to be the winning goal. Damn, once again a bad decision had cost us a goal. After another bad decision from the ref he eventually sent Monk off to the stand. What he'd done or said I've no idea, because he stands there with his hands in his pockets most of the time and only seems to get animated a few times. We did get a couple of great chances as Sacko kept getting plenty of space to run at them down the left-hand wing, but his final ball meant he either lost the ball or he should have passed to the middle for Wood to score but chose to shoot wide. The thing was, though, the team never gave up and kept going all game, so our fitness levels have improved. It was a shame we didn't get anything out of the game as we deserved a draw, and also didn't get that fifth game unbeaten in a row. At the end of the game the Leeds fans stood to applaud all the team, plus Monk, off the park as they headed to the tunnel to go under the stand we were in. The referee got a load of abuse thrown at him as he'd had a terrible game, and had also favoured the home side with some of the free-kicks.

I didn't feel too despondent because we had lost, as the team had never given up trying. Despite the fact we gave the ball away a lot and couldn't get the final good ball in, they were showing they wanted to get something out of the game, which is a big improvement.

After the game, we were still stuck in traffic and didn't get away until 11 p.m. due to a traffic light stuck at red! Is there any wonder I hate the colour red! Earlier in the day I'd been stuck at a red traffic light for a while then I saw a damned lone magpie. Now, I wasn't going to get superstitious, but that got the blame for our loss too. That saying, when we eventually got on our way we made good timing and, despite a quick services stop, got back to Leeds at 3.10 a.m. Finally in bed at 3.45 a.m., sleep still wouldn't come and then I was back up in a couple of hours to go to work. Even though we had lost last night, I couldn't help but whistle 'Marching on Together' over and over again once I'd got up! I managed to get through the day okay and only started falling asleep whilst typing this blog up! What with my computer updates taking hours and the falling asleep, it's taken me a lot longer than I wanted it to, so bang goes my early night!

We will have to pick up the pieces on Saturday with the visit to Elland Road of Barnsley, so here's hoping we can do just that. See you then LUFC – Marching on Together.

CHAPTER 4 – OCTOBER 2016

BARNSLEY – 1 OCTOBER 2016

Before I start my blog again, I want to pay my respects to Duncan Revie who has just died, the son of the best manager that Leeds have ever had. The name Revie will always be revered by me as I was privileged to have been around to see the best team ever play. My thoughts go out to his family at this sad time and there will be a minute's applause at the start of the game today.

I'd gone to the tip again before setting off for Elland Road, wearing my Leeds things as usual. A lad there at the same time asked if I went into the Peacock and I said yes. He then told me he'd be there himself later and would see me there no doubt. I then went to pick up my granddaughter Laura and had an unexpected trip to Leeds via the White Rose Centre, so that she could have her photo taken with the Stormtroopers at the Disney Store.

By the time we arrived at Elland Road it was already 2.30 p.m., so we had a quick visit to the Peacock before going in. I wanted to be in place for the minute's applause to take photos that I wanted to share with Duncan's son. I don't like getting to the ground so late, though, but there were plenty of fans around as over 25,000 fans were expected.

The team today was Green, Ayling, Bartley, Jansson, Taylor, Phillips, Sacko, Hernandez, O'Kane, Wood and Dallas. Subs used were: Antonsson for Sacko, Roofe for Hernandez and Vieira for Dallas. Attendance was 27,350 with 2,413 from Barnsley.

I'm pleased to say that Duncan got a fantastic send off from everyone and his family were stood on the side of the pitch clapping with everyone else. As I sit in the Kop I couldn't be sure for certain that the name Revie Stand is shown across the top of the stand. If it is, that is a long-lasting reminder that the name Revie will be part of Elland Road for eternity. Leeds started off well, but after a while we seemed to make hard work of it by playing quite deep and passing the ball across the back. Obviously Barnsley weren't going to make it easy for us but we needed to go forwards a lot quicker as our build-up was slow and predictable. There was a good atmosphere about the place, though, and eventually we won another corner but from the left-hand side this time. Our earlier corner had the same issues as usual, that we couldn't beat the first man. With this second one I think it took us all by surprise, as the ball came over and Bartley put it into the net! I can't remember the last time we've scored from a corner but was very happy to see this. The goal put us on the upper foot and although Barnsley had a couple of chances, we went into the break a goal up.

The second half hadn't been going long when we doubled the lead. This half was completely different to the first in the way we played. I said to the lad next to me that we'd been kidding in the first half as we'd come out all guns blazing. Hernandez got the ball and ran at the Barnsley defence and struck a shot that beat the goalie, going into the back of the net and sending the Leeds support into raptures. We had a few more good chances then we seemed to go off the boil for a while.

Barnsley H 1st October 2016

Barnsley H 1st October 2016

When we started playing deeper again, which meant we were inviting Barnsley to attack us, we had a lot of defending to do. Until they got one back, though, I wasn't too worried, but once they'd scored was hoping there was no way they'd get another one. With the Leeds fans in fine voice the team knew they'd got the support behind them. We defended really well though and managed to keep them out in the last minutes to get the three points and the win. It's a good feeling getting the three points, having a good atmosphere and knowing that the team are trying and playing well. I thought Phillips grew into the game having given the ball away a few times in the first half, but then made some great tackles along with O'Kane. I think our central defence has made such a difference to the team, with both Bartley and Jansson giving Green the support he definitely needs with their height. That said, the whole team are doing well, even though at times it doesn't always work, there is progress to be seen. It's a long time since we have seen this at Elland Road and long may it continue.

On the way back to the car, there was a large police presence around so I'm not sure if anything had happened as they seemed to be looking for someone. I thought maybe a group of Barnsley fans had been heading that way, but who knows? I'm sure someone will let me know if they saw anything!

I'll finish with a thought to my friend Sue and her husband Paul, who arrived at the ground with 20 minutes to go and just in time to see Barnsley score. Having been at the opposite end of

Barnsley H 1st October 2016

the country with a car that wouldn't start, the delay impacted on them getting to Elland Road for kick-off. They still got there which is what counts in the end, although the fact they put 300 onto the attendance was a bit much! First it said 27,050, then later on 27,350! It also reminded me of us travelling to Southampton in the seventies when our coach broke down at the services. We eventually got another coach which also broke down. By the time we got to the ground and into the stand there was about 15 minutes left, but we got there, which is what counts!

Back to the silly international break again next week. I would much rather that our far away games would be played on these days instead of midweek. Again, just as we start getting some momentum going this could have an impact on us. Hopefully, though, after the break we can carry on where we have left off! Fingers crossed. When I think back to Don Revie's team playing both for club and country (especially Scotland in those days), they played so many games in a short while. They never shirked from what they had to do and would put the national side's prima donnas to shame, who get over-pampered in my opinion. See you at Derby – LUFC – Marching on Together!

DERBY – 15 OCTOBER 2016

Last night as I listened to Noel Whelan on BBC Radio Leeds, I suddenly twigged that the Wigan home game was next Tuesday. Despite seeing it in my diary I'd no idea we'd got a midweek game! I then decided to look for my Derby ticket, only for panic to set in. I found my Wolves one for the week after, but couldn't find the one I wanted. I realised then that I'd left it a bit late to organise a replacement, but luckily I found the said ticket in my bag. Phew, what a relief! At least my dog hadn't eaten it like she did the last time I went to Derby, which meant I'd to pick up another one at the ground!

As I set off for Leeds I felt really upbeat and was in a happy mood. This was a lot different to how things had been only a short while ago, when I already knew the football wouldn't be up to scratch. Obviously, with the international break that may prove to be a blip again, but at least I was looking forward to my football once again. I started to reminisce about the seventies when listening to the Stylistics on the radio, and on leaving Billy's bar got my first picture of the day of the great man himself leading the team out.

We stopped at Chesterfield, where we headed to a different Wetherspoon's than usual, and was surprised to find loads of Leeds fans already in there. I think the pub knew we were coming, having all yellow and blue balloons hung up to welcome us.

We arrived at the ground about 30 minutes before kick-off and got up to get off the coach. We were told we couldn't get off yet as the police wanted a word. We were told there was a dog outside that would sniff out drugs and pyrotechnics, so if we had anything to leave it on the coach. We would have to walk past the dog too, but had to ignore it. We walked straight past without any issues and had our tickets checked near the turnstile. I was surprised when the steward tore off the

Derby A15.10.16

end of the ticket cos it had the bar code on it! The next thing was a bag search and I also had a body search. I don't think I've had such a deep bag search as today. What's that? My water. What's that? My books, I'm an author and always carry some with me. Okay I can see they are books. What's that? My blanket, aka banner! Et cetera, et cetera. My bum bag – What's that? My glasses. What's that? My phone. What's that? My money! At least the lady was pleasant enough but crikey, we were only going to a football game! I found out then why they'd ripped the barcode off my ticket – the turnstiles had broken! Inside another female steward helped me tie my banner up before I found my seat. There looked to be a sizeable crowd there today.

The team today was Green, Taylor, Bartley, Jansson, Ayling, O'Kane, Phillips, Mowatt, Sacko, Wood and Hernandez. Subs were Roofe for Sacko, Grimes for Mowatt and Antonsson for Wood. Attendance was 31,170 with 3,132 Leeds fans. Monk was sat in the stand today due to a one-game touchline ban.

The first half was one of those games again and wasn't really very good at all. I shouted to Hernandez that he should do something better with his balls! Well I knew what I meant, as his final ball lacked pace and was picked up easily by Derby. As the game went on we seemed to be defending really deep once again. I hate this because it means we are inviting the others to attack. Just before half-time, though, we actually upped the tempo and were very unlucky not to take the lead when Bartley's header from a corner hit the crossbar. Although Derby didn't look anything special, they had just got McClaren back as their manager which was sure to fire them up. I think we missed a trick not to get stuck into them a lot earlier than we did, as it gave them time to settle. By hitting the crossbar, we had just shown what could happen if we upped the tempo.

At half-time I saw Gary Edwards, who informed me that the Kippax lads will be playing the Norwegian Leeds fans at football the day before the Newcastle game, so I will make sure I get to watch them. It was a good day last time I saw them play each other. Also, I don't think the 'Caution very hot water' signs in the ladies were needed as the water was cold!

I was hoping that the second half would see us up our game, but it was Derby's sub who had only come on a few minutes earlier who scored for them to put them into the lead. We tried to change the game with some subs but Derby were seeing more of the ball now, and putting us under pressure. Green made a great save from them, but then they nearly scored a second. I wondered who the player was getting some stick off the Leeds fans, and when he put the ball into the net it was one of those déjà vu moments. I saw it was Ince and he was just going to saunter up to the Leeds fans to give some stick back. Unfortunately for him, the Leeds fans laughed back at him as the goal had been disallowed for offside! The ball hadn't been running kindly for us for most of the game and especially in the first half; the ref was letting fouls on us go and giving Derby free-kicks. A little bit more precision from us in our passing would have helped. Again, it wasn't until the end of the game that we put pressure onto the Derby goal. Although we never really looked like scoring from open play, we had one shot on target when a free-kick by Phillips was half saved by

Carson. During injury time, though, we all thought we had scored only to find out that a brilliant shot from Antonsson had hit the upright and bounced back into the penalty area. What a shame, as a point would have been a good result in my opinion.

We called into the ladies and then a few women tried telling this fella that he was going into the ladies' loos by mistake. He just shrugged his shoulders, ignored them and went into one of the cubicles. It hit me that one had been in at half-time too, maybe the same one? Sorry lad, but there's no need, just use the gents in future please. A load of fans were laughing at me as I was waiting for him to come out so we could get a photo to identify him. Eventually, after doing that, we headed out.

It was only a short walk to the coaches, as we found our way ahead blocked by the police and something was happening. We stopped where we were at the entrance to the car park, not knowing what to do. This Derby fan said it's always like this when Leeds are here, so I said what have we done? The next thing a woman stood behind me ended up on the floor. She told me after that she had been pushed over by a Derby steward for no reason. I can vouch for the fact she was stood there the same as I was, not doing anything. The next thing this young kid was stood to the right of me in a green shirt, he was grabbed by loads of stewards who looked as if they were taking him away. I didn't see anything untoward to warrant it, but the next thing someone (I assume it was his dad) shouted whoa, intervened and they eventually let him go. They still weren't letting us go through the cordon of police, but Sue had gone to the left of it all and managed to get through. I decided I was getting photos and then heard that some Leeds fans had been bitten by a police dog and some others had been hit with batons by the police. One lad who had been bitten came up to me so I could get photos of his bites. Others were telling me they'd been hit. I was then told that there was another lad who'd been bitten laid on the floor in front of the coaches just at the time the ambulance arrived. The police were trying to move everyone on and I said I needed photos, as others were saying, it was for evidence and I was the official photographer for the fans! I had seen a policeman with a dog and he looked like he was trying to sit on it to calm it down. Whether that was the biter I'm not sure, but in such a crowd of people this was out of order. Also, the police hitting fans with the batons were hitting out indiscriminately and a woman told me she had been hit on the back with one and sworn at. Unbelievable! She said they'd been singing and had asked why the police were hitting out at fans and got hit for it! Someone also said that some Derby fans had got into the middle of the Leeds fans and had been mouthing off and that's when it kicked off, with some Leeds fans reacting aggressively to this. Another told me that steward 416, I think it was, had been the one to start everything in the first place. One of the Leeds stewards had also been bitten and had his shirt ripped. The answer from a policeman was that the dog can't discriminate between a Leeds fan or a Leeds steward! He was challenged by a girl near me saying that it shouldn't be allowed to bite anyone in the first place! The lad on the floor from Scarborough looked in a bad way as he was helped to his feet to the ambulance. I was told later that he had a

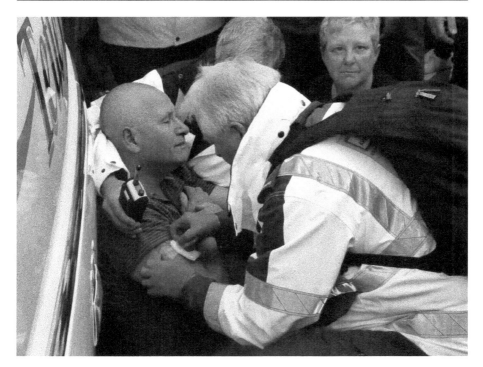

Derby A15.10.16

bad ankle too, and I only hope he is okay. These other lads, when I asked where their injuries were, couldn't tell me as they'd been hit and didn't really know what had happened. It looked like a bit of concussion to be honest. As well as the photos I got, there were plenty of videos being taken, so hopefully justice will prevail. The FSF on Twitter have already indicated they are able to help if needed and Jon Howe, one of the new committee members of the Trust, has also offered to help anyone caught up in the events. Whatever happens, the events after the game were way over the top and not needed. Eventually we got on our coach and set off home with an unexpected, unwarranted and unwanted end to the game.

With our home game against Wigan on Tuesday and then away to Wolves next Saturday, I'm hoping we can pick ourselves up to get some points. The team were trying today, though, regardless of misplaced passing, but it felt like a step backwards today. I don't like the international break and it was a shame it could have impacted on the momentum as we seemed to be heading in the right direction. Fingers crossed we can turn it around again. See you on Tuesday – LUFC – Marching on Together!

WIGAN – 18 OCTOBER 2016

There was a nip in the air and it felt icy, so I wasn't looking forward to being cold as we headed to Elland Road. We pulled off the M621 onto the roundabout and were the first in the queue as the

DUNCAN REVIE

1954 - 2016

traffic lights turned to red. How your life can flash in front of you in a matter of seconds turned to reality a few moments later. As the traffic lights changed I set off, and had got to the slip road going back up to the M621 only for a stupid idiot in a black car to come across the left lane that I was in at speed, missing my car by inches! It all happened so quickly but luckily my reactions were to brake, but we were left shaking our heads in astonishment at the idiocy of the lunatic and the close call. That was a nice start to the evening.

We stayed in the Peacock for a while and it was nice to meet up with Sean, who had been living in Australia and was now back living down south. As the nights are drawing in we headed into the ground in the dark, having the usual bag searches before getting into the Kop. There seemed to be a fair few fans around and there was a good atmosphere about the place despite us getting beaten by Derby on Saturday. As I stood on the steps to get my customary photos at the start of the game, people I knew stopped to talk to me, which ended up with a steward asking us to move on! Oops, I hadn't realised it was causing a jam as loads of fans were coming in right on kick-off. I said I would be taking my photos and then moving so was allowed to stay where I was.

The team today was Green, Bartley, Jansson, Taylor, Ayling, Hernandez, Wood, Sacko, Phillips, O'Kane and Roofe. Subs were Grimes for Sacko, Mowatt for Hernandez and Antonsson for Wood. Attendance was 19,861 with approximately 400 from Wigan.

I couldn't believe how warm it felt at the top of the Kop as there was no wind chill there, so luckily didn't need to put my big coat on. The game kicked off and there wasn't a lot to shout about, although both sides had a couple of chances. We had a shot on target from Wood and Green made a good save from one of the Wigan players. When we actually took the lead on the half hour mark the crowd had been getting generally frustrated, as once again passes weren't making their target and coming up short. As Sacko ran into the opposition, it looked like they had stopped him in his tracks, but as the crowd groaned, the ball rebounded for him. Sacko carried on running to the bye line and put a great cross in for Wood to volley the ball into the net to put us into the lead! We hadn't killed off Wigan, though, who came looking for an equaliser and hit the post before Green made a fantastic point blank save to deny them, then we cleared the second attempt from the rebound. That was very close but we went into the break in the lead.

I was hoping that in the second half we would go at Wigan and put them under pressure. At times it reminded me very much of the Derby game, as we were defending deep and looked like we were inviting Wigan to attack us. We also said it looked like we were trying to defend a one-goal lead instead of trying to add to it. We did manage an attack and Ayling's shot on target was put out for a corner. From the resulting corner it was a shame that Jansson's header was kicked off the line, as that could have made a difference to how we were playing. We had another chance with a Wood header that brought out a good save from the Wigan keeper. Despite the fact that there were still 20 minutes to go, we wanted Leeds to go for it instead of being very cautious in trying to preserve the one-goal lead. When we did put some pressure on it made a difference. Everyone around me couldn't understand why Monk had brought Grimes on to replace Sacko. It didn't make sense at all, as Sacko had been trying and had put some pressure onto the Wigan defence. I said that Hernandez was injured and Mowatt would come on for him, and also that Wood was limping too so Antonsson would probably come on to replace him. These latter subs both happened but it was the first sub that disrupted the flow of play which, although it wasn't brilliant at times, it did have an impact. Jansson was also limping too. Mowatt put some good passes in once he came on and it looked like we had a better shape, plus he was running all over the pitch at the time as well. Wigan hadn't given up, though, and when they got a corner in the dying minutes, they got the dreaded equaliser when the ball hit the crossbar but then the rebound was stuck into the net. That was the cue for disgruntled fans to leave the ground. We stayed until the end but it was a bitter blow that we couldn't get the three points and keep the clean sheet. It also felt like we had lost rather than drawn and got a point, which is better than nothing I suppose.

With another away game on Saturday at Wolves, we will have another hard game ahead of us. Fingers crossed we can get something out of that one! Before I end today, apologies for the lateness of the report, which was due to babysitting duties and proofreading my daughter's work. I will also be missing the Norwich Cup tie next week due to me having to travel to Guildford instead to see my daughter's final performance at Uni. For once, I have to put her first, but have other members of my family going in my place to the game. I hope to get some photos taken at the game, and if so I will post them on my return. I was being selfish in wanting us to have an away tie just so that we would play on the Wednesday and ensure I didn't have to miss the game! Unfortunately for me, it didn't happen.

Finally, I have just heard the news that Gary Sprake, our goalie from the Don Revie days, has died today. He was actually one of my heroes at the time and despite his errors that normally hit the headlines, he was a great goalkeeper and made some fantastic saves. I can always remember being at St Andrews, Birmingham where I was stood behind the goal and saw my friends Carole and Margaret throwing packets of chewing gum into the back of the net for Gary. Apparently they did this every game! The only thing that upsets me greatly was that Gary betrayed the team and Don Revie to give some interviews for money. I may not have been able to forgive him for that, but I wouldn't wish his death on his family. RIP Gary Sprake! See you Saturday — LUFC — Marching on Together!

WOLVES – 22 OCTOBER 2016

Before I start my blog today, I want to pay my respects to Helen Eyre and her family on this difficult day. Today marks the one year passing of young Leeds fan Skye Thompson who died suddenly aged 17. She will always be remembered by her family's brave decision to donate four of her organs to enable others to live. When I shared details of a request by her Uncle Scott for a minute's applause on 17 minutes at the Blackburn home game, I had no idea of the strength of social media. My post reached out to over a million people on Facebook and the family got their wish as the whole ground rose up on 17 minutes for the applause. Rest in Peace Skye, your legacy will live on with others, and a big hug to Helen and her family as my thoughts are with them.

Although it was dark when I got up, I was glad to see that it was daylight when I set off for Elland Road. I know I've said that I'm not going to be superstitious any more, but as soon as I saw that lone magpie waiting at the side of the M621 to see me, my initial thoughts were, well that's us losing today then! Obviously time will tell, and hopefully it will be the opposite, please.

Billy's bar was open for us to meet and there were only a couple of Fullerton Park members in, the rest were the Griffin Branch. They asked what time we were leaving and I said 9.00 a.m., which was same as them. They were heading for Tamworth before the game, although I wasn't too sure where we would go. As 9.00 a.m. approached I couldn't believe that there were relatively few of our branch members in, and I thought maybe I'd be travelling with the Griffin Branch! It was only as my friend Sue arrived and she told me that we were leaving at 9.30 a.m. not 9.00 a.m. that I realised I'd messed up! I'd ordered two lattes for us to take with us, and unfortunately by the time I'd seen Sue she'd already got one, so I gave the second one away.

On the coach we headed for Sutton Coldfield and the Bottle of Sack. Last time we were here it was an eventful visit as a robbery happened across the road whilst we were in the pub. In the pub, we were approached by a couple of men who had recognised our colours and said they were Leeds

Wolves A 22.10.16

supporters who had been watching Leeds in the seventies. We had a nice chat before they went on their way but as I've said before, wearing Leeds colours always gets people coming up to talk to us. Great for anyone lacking in communication skills!

We arrived at the coach park just before 2.30 p.m. and we started walking down with other Leeds fans to the ground. I caught up with some Leeds fans who had sustained injuries last week and had a chat with them before continuing to the ground. Although a Wolves fan had mentioned the police would be up for our visit this week, they were lower key than last week at Derby, I'm pleased to say. Searches were being carried out as usual before getting into the ground, where we were down the side. I put my banner across the back seats near where my seat was.

As we had come across the dual carriageway it took me back to the seventies, when we would have headed for the South Bank instead. That used to be such an imposing stand when it was terraces but it looks nothing like that now. In my book *Follow Me and Leeds United* I have made a few references to our visits to Wolves, with some terrifying times as a Leeds fan. I certainly don't want to go back to those times of football violence!

The team today was Green, Bartley, Taylor, Jansson, Ayling, Vieira, Sacko, O'Kane, Wood, Phillips and Roofe. Subs were Mowatt for Vieira, Cooper for Sacko and Doukara for Wood. Attendance was 23,607 with 2,452 Leeds fans. We'd sold all our tickets within a matter of minutes for this one.

As the game kicked off I'd come without any preconceptions for this game. As well as me seeing a lone magpie, Sue had seen one whilst I was asleep! We came under a bit of pressure in the first half and we were very lucky that the three times Wolves came close to scoring, one went over the crossbar and some great defending from Jansson and Bartley prevented them from taking the lead. When Sacko came close with a great opportunity his shot hit the crossbar. A chap next to me had said he couldn't score in a brothel! I said once he gets one it will open the floodgates! We were still playing deep and kept passing the ball back in defence, putting us under pressure and inviting Wolves to attack. I said as Monk was in the stand last week the same as us, he should see that our best form of defence is attack. O'Kane played some good stuff but also presented Wolves with a great chance when he passed back into the path of a Wolves player. Luckily for us, Green made a great save to prevent them scoring. At times we are our own worst enemy.

It was also a battleground out there with injuries and players going down left, right and centre from both sides. Our players, and Jansson and Bartley especially, were down for a time. It looked like Jansson is carrying an injury still and I was concerned that he wouldn't last the game, but he is made of stern stuff. Bartley had to change his shirt as he'd been bleeding. At times the ref was letting some things go, and as the Wolves fans chanted we only get shit refs I shouted they haven't a clue. I can remember a certain game, two days after the FA Cup Final in 1972; we were denied two penalties as Wolves players played pat-a-ball in the penalty area not once but twice! As we were discussing things amongst a group of us, one chap said that another lady and I should go into the

Wolves A 22.10.16

Wolves A 22.10.16

changing rooms at half-time and be manager, as we were putting the team to rights! It was funny, though, and gave us all a laugh. At least we went in on an even keel at half-time.

For the second half, I was glad that the sun wouldn't be so strong, I was glad to have my glasses that blocked most of the glare. As we were playing towards the right goal this time at least we wouldn't have that issue. We still were coming under the cosh at times, but it felt as if we were growing in stature. We kept fighting for the ball even when we lost it. We were on about keeping the team on the pitch as it was, and hoped Monk wouldn't make any changes to it as we were gaining momentum. This paid off when Sacko got the ball down our side and managed to get the ball past their defender. As I poised for the photo just as the ball hit the net, someone's arm went up in front of me so I reckon I missed it! I can't blame anyone for cheering, though. I'd like to know when the offside rule was changed, because the linesmen today didn't have a clue. When a Wolves player and their goalie are in front of our attacking player it is not offside. There was no way that our player had only the goalie in front of him, so for the linesman to put his flag up for offside only had us all shaking our heads in disbelief. As we made the substitutions we knew that we were going to have to defend to keep the lead and my only hope was that we could do it. Holding on to the lead is not something we can do usually, but on this occasion we did manage it. All the team, as well as the fans, were really chuffed at the end of the game and it was good to see. Jansson took his shirt off and gave it to a lad in a wheelchair and Mowatt threw something into the crowd.

It was a very happy set of Leeds fans leaving the stadium, singing away. Getting the three points is what matters and although we had come under the cosh a lot and it felt like Wolves would be the winners, Leeds had overcome all the odds stacked against us. As we got out of the ground there were a group of Wolves fans to the right of us who were getting moved back by the police. There had been an announcement over the tannoy saying that there would be restrictions placed on fans leaving the ground. As a few Leeds fans moved towards them they were moved back, and some of our fans were steering a lad out of the way that I knew. I went up to him and did my mother hen act and escorted him back to his coach to ensure he was okay!

As I said in my Wigan blog, I will not be at the Norwich Cup game on Tuesday so I won't be able to post a report and photos unless I get one of my other daughters to update me. You never know! I will still wear my Leeds shirt to Guildford as I go and see my youngest daughter do her final performance for her Vocal Degree. As much as I would love to be at Elland Road, for once I will have to put my daughter first. I will look forward to catching up with you all at Elland Road next Saturday for the Burton game. I've already arranged to meet one of the Irish lads for a photo in the Peacock. See you then LUFC – Marching on Together!

NORWICH, EFL CUP 4TH ROUND – 25 OCTOBER 2016

As mentioned, due to my youngest daughter Emily's final performance at University, a big thank you to my granddaughters Hannah and Laura, along with their mum, for taking some photos from this game in my absence. Hannah said that Norwich were massive cheaters and they scored, which was terrible. Because there had to be a winner in the EFL Cup it went to penalties and Leeds won. Both girls were buzzing and really enjoyed it because we won!

BURTON ALBION – 29 OCTOBER 2016

By the time I reached Elland Road today, I was later than anticipated due to an unexpected happening. By the time I picked my granddaughter Laura up, though, I had seen three magpies together so immediately thought we would win. When someone outside the ground had asked how we would do today, I had said I would take things as they come as I couldn't really predict the outcome. Burton, as newcomers to the division, wouldn't be an easy team to beat.

As we walked to the Peacock some Irish lads got out of a taxi so I ensured they got a photo, plus one of the Norwegian lads in the Peacock and some more Irish lads going into the ground.

The team came out onto the pitch and then I saw them getting together in the middle of the pitch for a minute's silence. At first I wondered what it was for, then the chap said over the tannoy as this was the last home game before Remembrance Day, we would have silence after the bugler had played the last post. At first all the fans burst into a round of applause after the bugler had finished, and then we had another minute's silence which was immaculately observed. I must admit that I wanted to cry at the end of this as it was so moving. To all those who died in the wars, these

Norwich EFL H 25.10.16

words that follow have my greatest respect: Age *shall* not weary them, nor the years condemn. At the going down of the sun and in the morning. *We* will *remember them*. RIP to all fallen soldiers.

The team today was Green, Ayling, Taylor, Bartley, Jansson, Sacko, Hernandez, Wood, Phillips, O'Kane and Roofe. Subs were Doukara for Roofe, Vieira for Hernandez and Mowatt for Sacko. Attendance was 24,220 with approximately 500 Burton fans.

Burton H 29.10.16

Although I only missed the Norwich Cup game due to travelling to Guildford with my daughter and her band to see her final performance for her Vocal Degree, it felt like I hadn't been to a game for ages! Although I missed a cracker of a game and a great atmosphere, I was very proud seeing my daughter Emily have a fantastic performance who completely smashed it on the night!

The scoreboard looked different today and I couldn't work out if it was broken underneath or not? The game kicked off and Burton immediately put us under pressure and showed me that we couldn't under estimate their team. Although the game didn't have a lot to shout about, one thing that was apparent was that the Leeds team would try back others up and also chase balls that they lost. There were quite a few misplaced passes that got some groans from the fans, but nothing too bad. Burton could have taken the lead but we cleared it off the line and then we came close attacking the goal at the South Stand. Burton came close to taking the lead when Bartley headed the ball to clear it, only for it to hit the crossbar and go out for a corner. As we shouted that he should be trying to score in the opposite goal and not an own goal, someone said he was trying to carry on from Tuesday when he had two goals disallowed. The referee and linesman were being too kind to Burton as they went down so many times and kept getting the free-kicks. Many fouls that should have been given to us were ignored, more often than not. One foul on Jansson, though, which wasn't given, did make me think when he looked up to see if he had got a free-kick or not! I hoped that he wasn't trying to pull the wool over the ref's eyes at that moment!

The second half carried on more of the same, as Burton came out fighting and put us under a lot of pressure. We were defending well and putting in some right tackles, though, and I felt that Ayling was having a storming game, especially in the second half. He was attacking well and putting in some great tackles. Once again something seemed to click once we got to the 60-minute mark as we started putting some pressure onto the Burton goal. The crowd were responding well too, but after one attack when we didn't get a foul someone threw a bottle onto the pitch from the East Stand. Doukara came on to replace Roofe and it wasn't long after that we took the lead. Doukara was put through with a great ball from Hernandez and he looked like he was going to score until he was brought down in the area. It was a cast iron penalty, and their player was lucky to get away with just a booking. Before Wood stepped up to put the penalty into the net another bottle was thrown into the penalty area. Why on earth would someone do that when it could have put Wood off by delaying the penalty? Come on Leeds fans, we are better than that, so please think about things, as we don't want to give anyone the chance to punish us again. Burton still didn't give up after going a goal down and they still put us under pressure, getting a couple of free-kicks just outside the penalty area. When they won a corner, I said we should keep someone up at the halfway line to take the pressure off the defence. As we defended well from the free-kick the players ran out of defence with the ball and Doukara was put through. As he bore down on the goal it looked odds on that he'd score, but it nearly didn't happen as he was bundled over. Luckily he got up and stuck the ball in the net to send the crowd wild! Just before Doukara put the result of the game beyond doubt, it looked like Burton would equalise and we'd have a draw. It was great to get the three points and there was a fantastic atmosphere at the end of the game. There was a very happy crowd and buzz as we left the ground knowing we'd been unbeaten in the last seven home games, which showed what a turnaround we've had in recent weeks. It hadn't been the best of games, but there had been a lot of end to end play and a lot of passion shown by the team, which was good to see.

As we headed to the car, a lone Burton fan was doing his best to antagonise the Leeds fans by singing loudly on his own. At one time in the past he'd probably have been put on his backside but luckily for him times have changed here! As he was getting some jip from some Leeds fans stood by Billy's statue he turned round and walked backwards, only to end up nearly falling over a couple of cones. This raised a laugh from the Leeds fans. He continued doing his one-man act along Elland Road and had some Leeds fans giving him some stick. Once he walked away from the ice cream van with a couple of mates, I took his photo again.

The next round of the EFL Cup draw was made and we have been drawn away to Liverpool. For many of us who have been to Anfield in the seventies, we have plenty of memories from there, plus the games in later years. I've written plenty of stories about visiting both the red and blue sides in my book *Follow Me and Leeds United*. It wasn't a pleasant experience many times for a lot of us, that's for sure. I'm sure it will be different this time and that we will get a good allocation of tickets. We will definitely sell this out very quickly as the interest in this game is phenomenal!

After the game, I headed to Bradford to a party. It was great to see so many familiar faces, some I hadn't seen for a long time. Tommy and Carol McGuiness have run the Bradford Branch of the Leeds United Supporters' Club for many years and it was a tribute to their devotion to the branch that saw a fantastic turn out to say happy birthday to Tommy. I said I'd mention Joe Murphy who said I can't be a proper Leeds fan as I haven't been arrested! I did laugh at this though, as I'm not going to change the habits of a lifetime to oblige!

Apologies for the quality on some of the photos I have taken. I did take my camera into the shop to check the zoom as I don't think it is focusing correctly. Typical, it worked perfectly there, but I had some issues with it again today. You could say I've overworked it! It is nice that we have no game midweek and have the away trip to Norwich next Saturday to look forward to. It will be an eight o'clock start from Leeds for us, which isn't too bad but it will be a long trip. See you all there – LUFC – Marching on Together!

CHAPTER 5 – NOVEMBER 2016

NORWICH – 5 NOVEMBER 2016

Before I start my blog today, I want to mention a couple of things. Firstly, as Remembrance Day grows closer with more silences before kick-off, I want to pay my respects to all those who we owe so much to. Even though my dad was on the opposite side in the war, he made sure that I was brought up right in acknowledging and remembering those who died making sacrifices for us.

Secondly, many Leeds fans know that I am an author of three Leeds United books but I'm sure there are thousands that don't. As Christmas is approaching and if you are wondering what to buy the football fan in your life, then think about these. My first book is called *Follow Me and Leeds United* which is based on the seventies and a diary I wrote at the time. I had seven years of not missing a game home or away, and went abroad to see the great Leeds United team under Don Revie. It is about a girl in a man's world but I think it would be of interest to any fan who went at that time, because every story in there is true. It tells about the troubles you had to endure to follow your team, which many fans can empathise with. My second book is *Once a Leeds fan, Always a Leeds fan* which covers some from my seventies diary and many times in between till a couple of years ago. Other fans have also shared their stories in there. My third book is co-authored with Andrew Dalton, called *The Good, The Bad and The Ugly of Leeds United, Leeds United in the 1980s*. With stats

Norwich A 5.11.16

and stories of those times it is another one that you can reminisce with. The feedback from the vast majority of readers has been overwhelmingly positive and I am very grateful to have the feedback from those who have already bought them.

Available on Amazon as a book or ebook, I would be grateful if you could share this with other Leeds fans or even fans of other clubs who may be interested in reading them:

https://www.amazon.co.uk/Follow-Leeds-United-Heidi-Haigh/dp/1780913087/

https://www.amazon.co.uk/Once-Leeds-Fan-Always/dp/1780913990/

https://www.amazon.co.uk/Good-Bad-Ugly-Leeds-United/dp/1780913680/

Today I faced my second long trip in two days, having travelled to Guildford yesterday to see my youngest daughter graduate, a very proud moment for us. As it was, when the alarm went off this morning I nearly jumped out of my skin. I was cold when I set off from home but the sun was rising and it looked like it might be a good day. We had left Guildford shrouded in fog so I'm glad we'd left that behind, although I was surprised to hear later that it had been raining where my friend Sue lived. Today we had some of the Bradford Branch of the Leeds United Supporters' Club travelling with us so we had a full coach. As we got a few miles down the road we found out that one of our branch members had been left behind, but luckily he'd managed to get on the Griffin coach as they set off slightly later than us.

As today was a day for chilling out ahead of a manic week that I am expecting at work, due to a big event I am organising for Thursday, I'm glad that I could switch off and slept on and off most of the way to Norwich, awaking when we arrived in Thetford for our pub stop.

As we looked for somewhere to sit, three men asked who we supported and then said we could have their table as they were leaving. Keith, who runs the Fullerton Park Branch, told us about the Dad's Army museum and statues that were not far away, so I decided I would go and get a history lesson after having something to eat. The one thing I like about the Wetherspoon's pubs we visit is the fact that they retain a lot of history in the buildings they have taken over. On entering the museum, I was asked for the first part of my postcode and when I said HX the chap immediately asked if that was Halifax, which of course was correct. As I walked in with my Leeds shirt and scarf on another chap said, 'Oh no Leeds United,' and I told him there was a coach load of us here plus a minibus. He said, 'That Billy Bremner,' and I responded with saying he was my hero and always will be. They were really nice people running the museum though and it's good to see such great memories in there. I also walked a bit further down by the river to see the Captain Mainwaring statue too. As I couldn't find my poppy that I'd bought recently I bought another one, as it is getting nearer to Remembrance Day on the 11th.

I got back to the pub, where I had a chat with one of the lads from the minibus. He'd been reading my book on holiday last week and had forgotten how bad things really were in the eighties. This is why memories are great and should be kept and shared. It turns out that he sits next to one of our branch members every week in the East Stand.

Norwich A 5.11.16

Just before we were due to leave, a Leeds fan we didn't know was asked to leave the pub due to sticking a Leeds sticker on the clock. Keith had to say he wasn't with us and apologised, as the landlady wanted to kick everyone wearing their colours out of the pub. As it was, she didn't and we left shortly afterwards anyway.

We arrived in the coach park in good time but I couldn't believe the prices coaches had to pay to park. Keith said they'd paid £22 and not the £24.50 that it stated on the notice, but that is extortionate. That's what being in the Premiership does to you! As we got off the coach there were three policemen and a policewoman there, who all met us with smiles and asked if we'd had a long journey. Luckily for me I'd slept most of the way so it hadn't seemed a long one. We had a short conversation with them but it was nice to feel welcome and a complete contrast to the way we were met at Derby recently.

As we walked down to the ground, a Norwich fan walking alongside me started to talk about the upcoming game. His name was John and he said that his team hadn't played well for a while and had been unable to have two halves where they played well in both. He said they missed Jonny Howson too, and whilst some of their supporters didn't rate him, John said you could tell when he was missing. I told him Jonny's brother travels with us to the games. He also said that being in the Premiership had meant they had kept too many prima donnas who weren't playing for the shirt any more. I said we'd been through that a lot in the past, and although we hadn't hammered any other team for a long time, it would be nice to think we could score a few goals. I took a photo of him outside the ground and bade him farewell as I started following some others off our coach around the ground. What a difference from the Carrow Road in the seventies, where you had to walk up a great many steps to get into the Barclay Stand. I can remember my first ever visit there, asking some women what the words were to the song they sang. It's funny how they have stuck in my mind ever since. On the ball city, never mind the danger, sing on now's your chance, hurrah we've scored a goal. Hopefully that's correct but I'm sure it will be pointed out to me if it isn't. In fact, the only time Norwich fans sang today was once after each of their goals. As we carried on around the ground, I wondered where we were heading, especially as someone directed one of our wheelchair users the other way. As Sue and I stopped, a Norwich steward asked if we were okay and she directed us back the way we came. It was nice again to be treated in a good way. Despite sniffer dogs waiting for us along with the customary searches we got inside relatively quickly.

Once in the ground, I headed into the seats and couldn't see any Leeds banners up anywhere. When I asked the steward at the front of the stand where I could put mine he said they normally were hung up right at the back of the stand. Unfortunately, I needed some tape to hang it up and not ties, so it stayed in my bag. A big thank you to the many people I spoke to today who said they enjoy reading my blog, especially as they can't always go to games. The feedback is greatly appreciated

The team today was Green, Jansson, Ayling, Bartley, Taylor, Phillips, Hernandez, Wood, Doukara, O'Kane and Roofe. Subs used were Sacko for Roofe, Vieira for Doukara and Grimes for Hernandez. Attendance was 26,903 with approximately 3,000 Leeds fans.

Norwich A 5.11.16

The game started with two elderly gentlemen from Norwich holding their poppy wreaths before the two-minute silence, which was impeccably observed inside the stadium. A Norwich fan shouted out because he could hear some fans underneath the stand making a noise coming into the stadium, who obviously weren't aware of what was happening inside. Leeds fans were still coming up into the stand at least seven minutes after kick-off with many standing in the aisles. It wasn't going to be an easy game today, especially as we had beaten them at Elland Road a couple of weeks ago in the EFL Cup. The Leeds fans gave the Norwich fans some stick about this. Whatever happened today, I wasn't automatically thinking we had no chance of winning the game and despite not having any thoughts about any scoreline, I was looking forward to a decent game. Norwich looked up for it, and in the beginning were putting lots of pressure onto the team and were being helped by the linesman closest to us, who couldn't keep up with play and obviously needs to have glasses. The amount of things he didn't see, what with the ball going out of play along the line more than once, and he had no idea of the offside rule, I think he needs to go back to school! I said to the lads in front of me that I wondered if the reason Doukara was playing and we'd changed tactics was because Norwich were looking to man-mark Sacko today. He did come on later as a sub, but it could have been. We did manage to put some pressure on ourselves and managed to get a great save out of their goalie to prevent us taking the lead. I said we needed to change our tactics, as

Norwich were attacking us in waves. They did take the lead on 24 minutes, though, after they'd won a corner I think. As the ball came into the middle we had one player on the goal line at the far post but none on the nearest one, and Norwich were able to force the ball over the line at the latter. Something I've said we need to go back to is having one player on each post, as in the Revie days with Billy Bremner and Paul Reaney. The amount of balls kicked off the line by those two players showed how sorely this tactic was needed. After Norwich had scored, for some reason a load of stewards came and stood amongst the Leeds fans on the aisles but all this did was antagonise our fans. A few times, though, they all came tumbling down the terraces and falling over everyone, which was reminiscent of the Kop when it was all standing. A few heated arguments started as some Leeds fans couldn't see as the stewards were in their way.

At half-time I was following the crowd very slowly down the terrace steps. As I got to turn down the tunnel I stopped for a few seconds to take a photo, only to have a Leeds fan shout 'move' to me in an aggressive manner. As he went around me, as he could have done anyway, he said we all want to get downstairs. I'm very sorry you had to waste 10 seconds of your time, but you know if you'd have had manners and asked if you could get past me, I would have obliged! As I went to come out of the ladies toilets, it was the first time I've seen a no entry sign and a one-way system! I chatted to a few more Leeds fans downstairs and was very sad to hear that Doug, who was Kev from Ripon's friend, had died in Antigua the other week which was a very sobering moment. Another Leeds fan who has been taken too soon. RIP Doug, and I'll have to look through my many photos as I know you are on them somewhere.

At the start of the second half a more senior steward was stood in the aisle and I said to him that the stewards being there earlier had caused a lot of antagonism, and he said that's why he was there. Sacko replaced Roofe in the 55th minute, and to me that was when the game changed, in my opinion. Although we had been working hard, backing each other up and kept chasing lost balls, we still needed a spark which is what Sacko did. Within two minutes we had equalised when we managed to win a corner. From this Jansson scored to spark off fantastic celebrations amongst the Leeds fans, although at that moment I hadn't realised he'd jumped into the crowd! I also bet the steward I'd spoken to would have wished he was somewhere else as he was pushed back down the steps from the celebrating hordes of Leeds fans! Sacko ran down the wing and with some great footwork and play between him and Ayling gave Wood the opportunity to put us into the lead. Cue once again fantastic celebrations amongst the Leeds fans. After the second load of celebrations, all the stewards disappeared from the aisles. The last few minutes of the game seemed to pass slowly, though, and two minutes from time Norwich equalised which was such a shame, as we had been playing well. One thing I noticed (I'm sure Monk has listened to me, lol) was Wood staying up at the halfway line, therefore drawing two Norwich players with him. We were coming out of defence with some fast, attacking football and putting Norwich under pressure. When they said there was going to be seven minutes of injury time, though, I was wondering if we could hold out

Norwich A 5.11.16

for a draw as we didn't deserve to lose. As it was, we went one better when we won a free-kick and Vieira smashed the ball long-range into the net for the winner. The Norwich fans' taunts of 2–1 and you f****d it up were sang back at them as the Leeds fans were once again celebrating with gusto. How long it seems since we were able to enjoy our football like it is at the moment. Seeing the team giving their all and joining in with our celebrations is good to see; playing for the shirt is all that we ask, and it is great seeing everyone being together once more. As the final whistle went, to know we had won and got the three points was fantastic. The atmosphere had been the best for such a long time with many varied songs today which I loved. The Pontus Jansson song had a second verse. Pontus Jansson's magic, he wears a magic hat, and if you throw a brick at him he'll head the f****r back, he heads it to the left, he heads it to the right and when we win the championship we'll sing this song all night! It was a great feeling at the end of the game that we could at long last be on our way back. It is still too early to be 100 per cent sure, but it was lovely to enjoy something that has been missing for a long while. Some Leeds fans were looking at the TV and then everyone was cheering, jumping around and going mental. The reason being that the table showed Leeds United in sixth position, something else that has not happened for a very long time. It is nice to have the chance to be positive and today was reminiscent of the good old days, and long may it continue.

Very, very happy Leeds fans going along the road to the coaches as we head into another international break once again. After this game, I think we are on Sky TV for eight games in the near future. It is time we have our own channel, and they might as well put us on every game but keep all the games at 3.00 p.m. on a Saturday. That would mean our worldwide support has the chance to see us but also all the travelling support are looked after. Hearing it has cost some fans £200 to change their arrangements for the Barnsley game, as there were no trains back after the game for our distance travelling fans, I can sympathise with them. My suggestion is a happy medium for them all.

The sell-out home crowd for the Newcastle game is the next game we look forward to, in a couple of weeks. With it being a Sunday noon kick-off there is going to be one hell of an atmosphere and one to look forward to. If anyone is trying to sell spare tickets at more than face value, though, shame on them! Leeds fans should look after other Leeds fans and help them out, and not try to make a quick buck as they have done in the past. I thought those days were gone.

See you then, LUFC – Marching on Together!

NEWCASTLE – 20 NOVEMBER 2016

As we set off for Elland Road it seemed such a long time since we'd had a game. With our last one being away from home at Norwich before the break for the internationals, the break had come at the wrong time for me. There again, I'd be happy to ditch the breaks as I think it messes up the momentum in the League. I'd also rather have it that any far away games are scheduled for a weekend instead of midweek.

Newcastle H 20.11.16

I decided to ignore the lone magpie that jumped in front of my car; I wasn't going to be superstitious today, was I? It took us longer to get off the roundabout at Elland Road than it did to come down the M621. I thought it was because the fans' coaches were arriving, but it turned out to be their team at 11.45 a.m. With my daughter and granddaughter we headed for the Peacock, which was packed out. With a sold-out crowd today I knew it would be a waste of time getting served, so didn't bother. Lots of our fans had picked today as one of their choices despite the game being live on Sky. There was a large contingent over from Scandinavia and Ireland, although there are a few of them that travel over regularly. So, Sky, please note that you will still get high viewing figures with a full crowd; although this isn't the end of the live games, with more to come in the next few weeks.

We decided to head into the ground earlier than usual and luckily for us the queues were very light. One thing I would like to take the club up on is why on earth are they stopping fans taking their bottles of drinks into the ground? Do they or do they not serve drinks in bottles in the ground? This is an absolute pointless exercise which only winds people up. Where is the respect for us as a support? When thousands don't do anything wrong, please do not look to cause issues when there haven't been any.

As it was 45 minutes to kick-off, I couldn't believe the last time I'd been in the ground this early. There wasn't even anyone sat on our row! Lots of fans had been looking forward to this game, although to me it was just another game, but I still hoped we could win. With Newcastle being relegated last season it was always going to be a difficult game with all the money they'd had, but if we go out with the right attitude then anything could happen. There was to be applause on the 11th minute in remembrance of Gary Speed, who played for both teams, and his parents were both at the game.

The team today was Green, Bartley, Taylor, Jansson, Ayling, Vieira, Phillips, Roofe, Doukara, Wood and O'Kane. Subs were Sacko for Doukara and Antonsson for Vieira. Attendance was 36,002, which for a full house was disappointing to see. Not for the fans who came, but when we had a capacity crowd in the past of over 40,000 it was a lot lower than expected. There were approximately 2,700 Newcastle fans there.

I loved the sound of the whole ground (apart from the 2,700), singing 'Marching on Together' at the start of the game. It is spine-tingling and I was looking forward to having a good atmosphere today, although recently, it is the smaller crowds that have worked better for that.

We lost the toss and had to change ends, which wasn't a good sign. I couldn't remember the last time this had happened, either. Within 10 minutes of the start of the game, though, the referee showed he had his colours nailed firmly to the Newcastle mast. As well as giving them loads of free-kicks, some for next to nothing, he was letting fouls on us go unpunished. Unfortunately, that always means the opposition go from strength to strength.

As it was, right from kick-off we were put under pressure as Newcastle tried to make their recent Premiership experience tell. We kept giving the ball away and couldn't seem to get a grip

Newcastle H 20.11.16

on the game. Newcastle were quick on the ball and not giving our players time, so many mistakes occurred. On the 11th minute all the ground stood in unison for the applause for Gary Speed, which was good to see. Green made a good save from one of their players at a time when we seemed to be holding our own. Newcastle then took the lead: I didn't see the actual lob, but saw Green back pedalling to his line as he'd been caught off it. He went to catch the ball but dropped it, only for their player to get to it first to put the ball into the net. His lack of height probably told, but he should have tipped it over the bar rather than try to catch it. Damn, that sinking feeling appeared because it seemed to come out of the blue, despite their pressure. It also put us on the back foot for the next 10 minutes at least. It also told on the atmosphere too, as that familiar feeling of having the stuffing knocked out of you occurred.

Just before half-time, though, we had our best spell of the game and put Newcastle under loads of pressure, winning a few corners in a row. I didn't see the actual handball that occurred in the penalty area as the ones in front of me raised their arms, but everyone was adamant we should have had a penalty at that stage. Getting that was the difference between getting a grip on the game, but unfortunately for us the ref ignored our pleas and booked Jansson for his protests. This means he has reached five bookings so will be missing next week at Rotherham. The nearest we came was a header from Ayling that their goalie pushed over the bar. As it was, half-time came at the wrong time for us as we had upped the pressure, and a few more minutes may have given us a chance to equalise.

Newcastle H 20.11.16

As the second half kicked off, when we were attacking the South Stand we had a great chance to equalise, but their goalie saved the shot. After a while, it became apparent that we were struggling in midfield. I shouted that Monk should change it as I couldn't really see what tactics we were using. The one thing which I hate is the passing back to the goalie. This constantly puts us under immense pressure, especially when Green took such a long time with one clearance, that the Newcastle player was almost on his toes. They soaked the bit of pressure up from us but then seemed to waltz through our players, and a cross came to their player in the box on his own to put them two up. It shouldn't have been game over at that time, as we should not have been scared of them, but we couldn't get any great momentum going and you couldn't see us scoring. The feeling was that if we got one, we would get another, but it was one of those games where you knew it wouldn't happen.

At the end of the game many clapped the team off but I was frustrated with it all and didn't feel like it. I thought Monk's tactics hadn't worked and didn't think he'd done enough to change the game with his subs. Yes, I know Newcastle were top of the League, but to be honest, I felt we gave them too much respect and didn't keep the pressure on them enough. It reminded me of Leeds winning at Old Trafford in the FA Cup. Everyone was expecting us to get beaten but I said if you go with that attitude, then you will be. That's why they managed to win at home so many times as teams were beaten before they got there. It's only the last few games that we seem to be passing back to the goalie again all the time, but our best form of defence is attack. After the win at Norwich, which was fantastic, today it was back to reality and normal service resumed. In this division, though, anyone can beat anyone so we just have to pick up the pieces and get as many points as we can.

As we play Rotherham away in the teatime kick-off next week, we will find ourselves on TV once again. Fingers crossed that we can get over the suspension of Jansson and injury to Hernandez, but please Monk, no square pegs in round holes! We need to play to our strengths and play our players in their best positions. I know it doesn't always work with the squad but it is telling in the way we play when we don't.

As we headed back to the car we found ourselves surrounded by approximately 15 lads in Stone Island/dark clothes. When one said in a thick Geordie accent are you a Leeds fan, but not to anyone in particular, then why aye man, it took me back to the seventies immediately. Although they didn't say anything to us and were just going past, I remembered the incident at St James's Park when my friend Carole and I were chased by lads with knives on the way back to the coaches. Straight away the trepidation appeared as I tried not to start shaking. It may have been 40 years later, it may be nothing was going to happen, but it doesn't take long for those old fears to appear. I was glad they carried on up Elland Road as we went to the car because whatever happens, I'd rather be surrounded by our own fans and not the opposition!

See you next week, LUFC – Marching on Together!

ROTHERHAM – 26 NOVEMBER 2016

Before I start my blog today, it looks like my ambition of getting recordings of the Leeds fans singing our old songs is going to happen. I am in the process of getting all the songs I know put down on paper, together with some other Leeds fans who have wanted to do this for years too. We will be getting lots of our singing fans together (on a day to be arranged in the near future) so this can be achieved. The aim is to get the atmosphere back at Elland Road for every game and not just some. I am looking forward to working together with our fans to achieve this. Watch this space!

I wasn't looking forward to the cold today, as I woke up to freezing fog and temperatures just below zero. I was leaving just before midday as I wanted to go into Leeds first, but couldn't believe that my car was still iced up! I left home in bright sunshine as the fog had disappeared but it didn't last long, because by the time I got to Shibden the conditions deteriorated rapidly. Leeds was shrouded in fog too as I went to the park and ride. It's not often I'm at that side of the ground, so I took the opportunity to take a photo.

After a quick trip to the new John Lewis building and the German Christmas Market, I got back to the ground to take advantage of the 20% off in the club shop. Billy's bar beckoned before catching the coach. Luckily the fog had lifted as we neared Rotherham and pulled up outside the ground. We had both tickets and season tickets checked before the usual bag search with a row of stewards. To be fair, I was able to have a laugh with the steward before I made my way to the turnstiles, where a couple of the Leeds stewards who I knew were stood. They said hello to me and asked if I was at the right turnstile. As I said yes, the girl steward asked to check my bag. I said they'd just checked my bag back at the start and she was going to let me through, when all of a sudden this big bloke said it wasn't up to others to check bags but them! Some sort of security I think, but what a jobsworth! He was downright rude, what's this, what's that? When I said my banner, has this been checked so I said no. Get it out then so I can look at it. Has it got a flame retardant label on it? No, I said. Well you can't take it in. When he asked for the fire retardant paperwork, I handed it over and once he looked at it handed it back to me without saying a further word. I know trouble has always followed me around, but me being a troublemaker? Come on, where is the common sense? At least I got my banner hung up with the other ones in front of the disabled area, and thanks to Keely and others for helping out with tying them on to the bar for us.

The team today was Green, Taylor, Ayling, Cooper (in for Pontus as he was suspended), Bartley, O'Kane, Wood, Doukara, Sacko, Roofe and Phillips. Subs were Dallas for Doukara, Antonsson for Roofe and Berardi for Sacko. Attendance was 10,513 with 2,277 Leeds fans.

Once I'd heard that Rotherham were bottom of the League (as I don't normally take any notice of where the opposition is in the table) I thought immediately that today wouldn't be a pushover. Also, I'd heard Chris Wood say that he wanted us to come out like we did against Newcastle last week. My reaction to that was, what? We were scared of Newcastle and gave them too much respect! As it was, after we'd kicked off Rotherham had a couple of fast forwards so I knew it wouldn't be easy.

There was a long stoppage as one of the Rotherham players got treatment and then went off. But it was Leeds who took the lead as Charlie Taylor went on a run down the left-hand side. He crossed the ball into the centre and as it came to Wood in acres of space, you just knew it was going in the net! 1–0! That was a nice surprise as it was only 15 minutes into the game, plus it was from open play. Rotherham put the ball into our net but the whistle had already blown with the linesman having his flag up. The Rotherham goalie had treatment when he saved a shot and got treatment too. As play resumed and Leeds were defending at our end, a Rotherham player punched Cooper and was immediately given a red card and sent off. Before half-time the Rotherham goalie went off injured too. The rest of the half seemed to go on for a long time and wasn't very exciting, but at times Rotherham showed they could put us under pressure even with 10 men. With all the injuries seven minutes of injury time was added on, and I went and stood at the end of the row, ready to go downstairs at half-time. The next thing we had another attack and Doukara put the ball into the net to give us a two-goal lead at half-time.

Four men got lost in the ladies loos as they came in one after the other. I couldn't believe my eyes and only the last one walked out again when I shouted at them. It was very cheerful down below the stands, though, as there was a great sing-song about Pontus's magic hat! As it had got very cold before half-time at least it warmed everyone up.

It was hoped that we would go on and get a few more goals in the second half but although we had plenty possession, we couldn't get a further goal, although we did come close a couple of times. We didn't go for the jugular, though, and there was one shot from Rotherham that I was convinced had gone straight into the net with Green stranded, but luckily it had gone wide. This should have set the alarm bells going for us, though, as it wasn't us with 10 men, was it? To be honest, we did look comfortable for a lot of the time but I think the substitutions changed everything and not for the good. Whatever shape we did have disintegrated and you could see Rotherham getting on top. It came as no surprise to many of us when they pulled a goal back. The nerves set in then, as it looked all on that Rotherham were going to come back and get another goal. As they put us under immense pressure, there was a frantic goalmouth scramble as we somehow managed to keep the ball out and prevent them getting a draw. Phew, the final whistle couldn't come soon enough for us and it was a relief to hear it blow. Three points is the main thing and whilst we were in control for long spells in the game, we could so easily have thrown this away. Rotherham hasn't been a good hunting ground for us over the years so it was good to get the win, although it didn't feel like one at the end, just sheer relief that we hadn't been beaten. We did have calls for a clear penalty, though, when our player had his feet taken from him in the penalty area.

It felt weird coming out of the ground with it being a 5.30 p.m. kick-off, but at least we got home at a decent time. Tuesday sees us head for Liverpool for the next round of the EFL Cup. I

can't remember the last time we went there but we should remember from past times, they are nothing to be scared of. Go with the right attitude and play our best by not giving up is all that is asked. We are the underdogs but anything can happen. Although Don Revie and Bill Shankly had the greatest respect for each other, there were some great battles on the pitch. We were always called dirty, but our players were no dirtier than Tommy Smith who played for Liverpool. When Leeds won the League there in 1969 they got a great reception from the Kop, which was a great gesture. It was never a good place to go to as a Leeds fan in the seventies, though, which I have written about in my book *Follow Me and Leeds United*. Hopefully those times are long gone and I am looking forward to going back and seeing how things have changed. See you on Tuesday – LUFC – Marching on Together!

LIVERPOOL, EFL CUP 5TH ROUND – 29 NOVEMBER 2016

As soon as the draw was made for the next round of the League Cup, as I still call it, it was obvious that tickets would be like gold dust. I'm so glad that I've got the automatic away Cup tickets in place because I don't think I could have coped with the stress!

As it was, there were loads of fans trying to get tickets and we were sold out within minutes of them going on sale, leaving many disappointed. As I prefer to see the game live rather than watch it on the TV, I know how gutting that would be.

To make things easier for me and my daughter, we arranged to be picked up at Junction 25 of the M62 so that we could go after work had finished. We were there at the arranged time and stood at the bottom of the slip road near the roundabout. Just as we were expecting the coach to arrive, I noticed a police van had pulled up at the edge of the road on the roundabout. I realised then that a policeman was coming to talk to us, oh no! I walked straight up to him and he asked why we were stood on the slip road and I said we were stood on the path at this side of the sign. He then asked if we were being picked up there and said that if anyone stopped to pick us up on the slip road or roundabout they would be getting a fine and three points on their licence. There were cameras all over and that's how we'd been seen. There was no way I would let anyone suffer that fate, so we set off to move away to a safe place to be picked up. At that moment we heard another police car heading our way, but apparently there'd been a bump on the roundabout. As the coach pulled up at the bottom of the roundabout, I had to ring my friend Sue on the coach and the policeman told us to get picked up at the lay-by heading towards Huddersfield. As soon as we went that way I realised I'd made a mistake, as I should have told the coach to go towards Brighouse and get picked up at the lay-by there. It never rains but it pours as we got in a traffic queue all the way to Cooper Bridge and then had to go back to the motorway. It put approximately 15 minutes on to the journey which wasn't good, as the traffic had been bad on the way there. I always say that trouble follows me around and I wish it wouldn't! That wasn't the end of the traffic problems though, as we more or less got stuck in slow moving traffic straight away. We heard that there had been a crash at Ripponden which had blocked the road both ways, with the air ambulance called to take someone to hospital. We had toyed with the idea of being picked up at Junction 22 and were glad that we had decided against it. Our driver took a detour and we eventually got back onto the M60, but we still had issues there and on the M62. In fact, I would say we had traffic issues all the way; from the coach setting off until we arrived at Anfield it had taken us three and a half hours. Unfortunately, it meant we had missed a lot of the build-up to the game, but I was just glad in the end that we'd made it because we'd heard there had been a big accident on the M62. Apparently near Birch services both sides of the M62 had been closed. We heard later that some Leeds fans had been turned back, but obviously I don't know that for certain. So long as everyone was safe, that would be the main thing, but gutting if they didn't make it there. It had taken some of our southern fans four hours to get there so they did better than us going.

As we approached Anfield I noticed familiar parts of the road, the dual carriageway and the park (we always used to get bricked in the seventies at the end of it once the police escort had left us), Goodison Park and parking on Priory Road. Stanley Park, and remembering that I would never go over it because the Liverpool fans would always be waiting to batter the Leeds fans or worse, in some cases slash them with Stanley knives. I remembered the car park on the way to the Anfield Road End and having kids ask to look after your car for a payment. I paid at that time, but someone parking next to us didn't and had everything taken out of their van by the time they returned to it. Whilst hating having to do it, I knew it was the best thing to do under the circumstances. It was never a good ground to visit as a Leeds fans in the seventies because not only did we have the Liverpool fans to contend with, but they often joined forces with the Everton fans. All these things have been written in my first book *Follow Me and Leeds United* and it actually makes me scared reading the true stories from that time. As it was, I hoped that those days were long gone and that our visit today would be without incident.

We got into the ground just before the teams came out. Having stood on the Kop as a Leeds fan, which is also mentioned in my book, I had to take a photo of the bit behind the goal which is where we were stood. It's a lot different with seats in it, though. Their new stand was impressive, and to be honest, when looking at some of the grounds we've visited over the years, it was one of the better ones.

The team today was Silvestri, Berardi, Bartley, Cooper, Vieira, Sacko, Roofe, Taylor, Doukara, O'Kane and Dallas. Subs used were Phillips for O'Kane, Ayling for Cooper and Wood for Dallas. Attendance was 52,012 with 5,352 Leeds fans.

I knew it wouldn't be easy for us today, especially as Liverpool seem to have found their way again and are near the top of the Premier League. What I did say, though, is that as long as they go out with the right attitude and give all they can, then that is all that is asked of the team. Showing they care by giving their all and putting the same amount of effort in that the fans do day in, day out goes a long way to getting us all on the same wavelength. Despite the way things have been

NORWICH CITY 1-2 LEEDS UNITED

BRADY 24' 57' JANSSON

74' WOOD

prior to our recent spell, the Leeds fans have shown their loyalty in numbers time and time again. We had nothing to lose today as we were the underdogs and could go out and enjoy ourselves on the pitch and on the terraces.

Before the kick-off, a minute's silence was held for the football team from Brazil, Chapecoense; only six of the passengers and crew, including three players, survived a plane crash as they were on their way to a Cup Final. It was so, so sad and a horrible thing to happen to them all. RIP to them and thoughts with the families of all who perished.

Just before kick-off, the Liverpool fans started singing 'You'll never walk alone'. Personally, I was singing along with it (my friend Sue did too) before joining in with 'Marching on Together' with the Leeds fans. I always find it very moving as it was also a song we sang regularly in the seventies with our scarves held aloft, plus it was a song my dad had as his funeral song. Our best ever 'You'll never walk alone' was against Manchester City in the FA Cup at Elland Road, when we scored near the end of the game. Nothing will ever match that again, plus I climbed on a barrier too, which are long gone! To be honest, after that rendition, the atmosphere at Anfield from the Liverpool fans was very poor.

Leeds could have taken the lead in the first few minutes if Sacko would have managed to put his chance away, but sadly the goalie got to save it. I think he took one step too many but it was a case of having to take your chances when they are there. The Leeds fans were in full voice and it was a fantastic display all through the game, getting behind the team. Silvestri made a fantastic save to deny Liverpool from taking the lead a short while after. We actually started to play very well after the first initial moments, and the team were backing each other up and getting stuck in. We had to be careful as Liverpool had some really fast players and would counter-attack. The one thing we have started doing recently which infuriates me is the passing back to the goalie. The amount of times we have done that, which immediately puts us under pressure, is the only gripe I have, though. Our best form of defence is attack so please Monk, get that bit changed! Just before half-time we were really on top of the game and putting them under pressure. I was really enjoying the display from the team, which had everything: guts, playing some great football and putting some great tackles in and letting Liverpool know we were there! Going in 0–0 at half-time was very satisfying.

In the second half, we thought we had scored when Roofe sent a curling shot into the penalty area with the goalie beaten, only to see the ball come back into play by hitting the upright! What a goal that would have been and such a shame Roofe didn't get his just rewards. O'Kane had been injured in the first half, then we'd lost Cooper at the start of the second, but Ayling was a credible centre-half and played really well. Apart from some of the passing going astray and the going backwards rather than forwards, we showed we could play against a good team. In fact, if we'd have taken those chances, we maybe could have sneaked a win. As it was, we ran out of steam and Liverpool scored twice on the 76th and 81st minute to win the tie, which was disappointing but not unexpected. As soon as the ball hit our net there was an immediate cry from the Leeds fans getting behind the team. Wood managed to get the ball into the net but was flagged offside. Not as bad as the one in the first half, when there was no way we were offside. There has been talk that we were in our own half when the flag went up? Put it this way, though, the amount of linesmen who don't seem to know the rules is astronomical!

All I can say at the end of the game is that I am proud to be a Leeds United supporter. The way the team played as a team and battled well is looking good for the future. The fans got behind them the whole night and showed the world what they are missing by seeing us singing and chanting! As long as we have stability, that is the key. Many fans were saying the Cup isn't important and we need to concentrate on the League. I disagree, as winning breeds winning. It was also a chance to get into Europe (as long as that part hasn't changed!)

Our trip home was a lot quicker and I did my good deed of the day by dropping a lad off our coach in Mirfield. He had got off the coach at the same time as us and was going to ring a taxi. Well, I'm not the sort of person to leave someone stranded, and would rather know they got home safely. Once home, I realised I'd got a migraine starting and went to bed with one and got up with one this morning. Having only five hours' sleep before work wasn't good, but it is the price I have to pay to follow my team.

We have another game live on Sky on Saturday, with the 5.30 p.m. kick-off against Aston Villa. After today's showing against Liverpool, our team has shown they have no need to fear any other team. Go out with the right attitude and we can beat anyone on the day. Another three points would be great, so fingers crossed. See you there – LUFC – Marching on Together!

CHAPTER 6 – DECEMBER 2016

ASTON VILLA – 3 DECEMBER 2016

Although the kick-off wasn't until 5.30 pm today, we set off early as I was going to the LFU meeting first and my husband was going in corporate hospitality. What I will say is that Leeds United totally outclassed Huddersfield Town in the hospitality stakes, so well done! On the way to the Peacock, I met Paul who was buying my third book which was co-authored with Andrew Dalton called *The Good, The Bad and The Ugly of Leeds United*, and a big thank you to him for the support. When I got to the Peacock, I had a chat with a lad doing some research for his dissertation about the eighties and the impact the Premier League has had on football. It was good to chat and he had quite a few takers to put him in the picture.

We decided to go in early again as there was a big crowd again today. I followed my daughter and granddaughter to our seats but didn't check the row. It's a good job we woke up and got into our rightful row!

As I was taking photos of the mascots, they were interviewed on the big screen. One said his favourite player was his dad. Then the commentator said, and your dad is Ross McCormack (he now plays for Aston Villa but doesn't seem to be in Steve Bruce's plans). Layton said Leeds would win and was a mascot for Leeds; bless him, but good to hear that he's been brought up right!

The team today was Green, Ayling, Bartley, Jansson, Taylor, Vieira, Phillips, Roofe, Sacko, Wood and Doukara. Subs used were Dallas for Doukara and Mowatt for Roofe. Attendance was 32,648 with approximately 3,000 Villa fans.

After waking up yesterday to Pontus's magic hat going round and round in my head and then bursting into song, it's surprising how happy it made me feel. It's a good feeling to have, and despite the defeat at Liverpool, the fact we hung on until the 75th minute before they scored against us, we put up a fight and took it to them in their own backyard. I couldn't have been prouder to be a Leeds fan this week and long may this feeling continue!

Today we were up against Aston Villa, who are another of the clubs relegated from the Premiership last season. I don't reckon any game is easy in this division, but anyone can beat anyone on their day. After our display at Anfield, we don't need to fear anyone and as long as they go out and play their best, that is all that I ask. There was a minute's applause for the Brazilian team killed in a plane crash last week.

For most of the first half Villa had a lot of the ball and continued to put us under pressure. They made things quite difficult for us but I wasn't expecting it to be easy. The team kept plugging away, though, as we had a couple of chances not on target but it wasn't good to watch. As usual, we had some strange decisions from both the referee and the linesman to our left. I was glad to hear the half-time whistle, though.

The second half carried on much of the same, with Villa putting pressure on us and Green pulling off a couple of saves. There was one chance they had where I was certain they were through with just Green to beat, but luckily we managed to get the ball away. When Jansson was booked, a large amount of people around us just stared in disbelief. I know I'm biased but there was at least a dozen of us in agreement that it looked like he'd gone flying after a tackle but got up and carried on. According to a tweet on my daughter's phone, it said he'd dived! I'd have to see it again but it didn't look like it from where we were stood in the Kop.

Then Leeds took the lead, Roofe was bearing down the middle of the pitch towards us and a great cross from Doukara came in. I just knew Roofe's head was going to connect with the ball and score! He certainly did, and sent everyone into raptures. I'd answered his tweet last week when he was asking when he would score. I said that it would come in time; well it did, and it wasn't a long wait either. A fantastic atmosphere together with celebrations on the terraces was brilliant. Just before Roofe scored the whole ground was singing Pontus's magic hat (apart from the Villa fans of course), which obviously gave the team the boost they needed! Pontus went round getting the crowd going, and we didn't need much persuasion. Villa had a chance to get back into the game but luckily for us they didn't. I had been discussing the amount of injury time there would be with the chap next to me, and we were right with five minutes. I looked at my watch with a couple of minutes to go and then we killed the game off when Sacko came racing towards the goal and managed to get his foot in front of the defender to get a shot in. This slowed the ball down, and I was just going to get a great picture of it going into the net when Wood was going to make sure it went in, but someone jumped up in front of me so I missed it! The Leeds fans went wild, as we knew then that the game and the three points were ours!

There are some new vibes about the place. After capturing Radrizzani on my Newcastle photos that got lots of publicity, whatever is going on behind the scenes, we seem to have stability and are enjoying our football once again.

Next week sees us travel to Brighton before facing Reading and Brentford at Elland Road. I will continue to take each game as it comes but as usual just want as many points as possible. It is the first time in years we haven't had the season written off by October/November, so I am looking forward to seeing where we are in the next couple of months. For now, I will relish the moment and savour it all. See you next week – LUFC – Marching on Together!

BRIGHTON – 9 DECEMBER 2016

Firstly, I want to pay my respects to the family of Billy Bremner on the anniversary of his death two days ago. Billy Bremner always was and always will be my hero. He epitomised what being Leeds is all about and instilled in me the love and loyalty of supporting my team. You will never be forgotten.

Despite today's game being rearranged again for Sky TV, we were looking at a good following once again. To get there in time for kick-off meant it was straight there, and thanks to those fans who once again helped and looked after me to achieve this. You know who you are!

Brighton A 9.12.16

Inside the ground just before kick-off there was a great atmosphere below the stands. Thanks to Rawcliffe White for buying my co-authored book *The Good, The Bad and The Ugly of Leeds United* from me, which is appreciated. As I walked into the stand to go and put my banner up, I couldn't believe how slippery the steps were. I wasn't sure if they'd been washed recently as they were still wet, but it was quite dangerous underfoot and a health and safety hazard. Luckily, I made sure I trod gingerly to ensure I didn't end up flat on my back!

I was hoping that we'd be able to break our bad run of results here. The team today was Green, Taylor, Bartley, Jansson, Phillips, Vieira, Sacko, Roofe, Wood and Doukara. Subs were Dallas for Doukara, Grimes for Sacko and Cooper for Jansson. Attendance was 28,206 with 2,736 Leeds fans.

From the start, we were put under pressure from Brighton and they kept whipping in some dangerous corners that had Green and our defence flapping. It was always going to be a tough game but maybe we had the wrong tactics from the start, as we didn't really settle into the game. The referee, though, right from the start of the game set out his credentials early on and showed his true colours by booking two of our players, Ayling and Jansson. Brighton showed they'd been in the Premiership recently too, by diving all over the place and conning the referee very easily. I hate cheats!

114

On 20 minutes I cast my mind back to last season, when we were four goals down by half-time in an atrocious game from our point of view. I didn't want this timing to be significant, but unfortunately a couple of minutes later it did become that. Brighton had another attack and I thought they'd scored, but it looked like we'd kept the ball out. Then I thought we'd been given a free-kick as it was difficult to make out what had happened from the far end of the pitch. As the Brighton fans cheered, I saw one of our players walking to the tunnel having been sent off, damn! I couldn't see which player it was and had to work out from the ones left on the pitch that it was Phillips. To say I've got new glasses recently this didn't bode well! Brighton scored from the resulting penalty to put them into the lead.

After the sending off we had to regroup, with Doukara going into the midfield. We weren't playing at our best but we certainly didn't give up, and whilst they had only the one-goal lead it gave me hope that we could still turn things around. Maybe we also settled down a little bit more into the game at this time. Phillips would have also grown into the game in my opinion, if he would have stayed on the pitch and we'd had 11 men, then anything could have happened. As it was, we went into the half-time break still with the penalty between the teams.

At half-time I managed to catch up with big Mick Hewitt. Having already spoken to Tony and Gary Edwards from the White Rose Branch and also Collar (leader of the Kop), we are all in the process of getting the background in place for the recording of all the old Leeds songs. It had been my ambition for years to do this and I knew this was shared with the others. When we have

Brighton A 9.12.16

got things organised with the songs, then likeminded Leeds fans who want to be involved for the recording will be able to send me their email address. Singers will be required but those who know the majority of the old songs will also be needed. Watch this space! As we were stood there talking, all of a sudden a big boom-like bang went up, nearly making me jump out of my skin! That was the signal for loads of our younger fans going 'mental'. I love the singing and chanting though, and the Pontus songs just give off a happy glow in me.

During the second half, despite only having 10 men, I thought we kept Brighton out by limiting their chances. We didn't have many chances ourselves but one chance came to Wood off someone else, and it was such a shame he didn't connect with it to put it into the net. That was probably our only real chance on the night but it would have been a great equaliser.

The Leeds fans had a great second half with a constant over and over again of: 'Last Christmas I gave you my heart but the very next day you gave it away, this year to save me from tears I'll give it to Pontus Jansson'. This was absolute class and I loved this part. This went on until the last 15 minutes of the game and despite us being a goal down, we had shown how to support our team with good humour. Then we had the rug pulled out from under us when the ref awarded Brighton a second penalty. They had attacked the goal in front of us when their player went down on his knees with ease and conned the ref, but I am adamant that in no way should this penalty have been given. I couldn't comment on the first one as I'd need to see the replays, but have been told that decision was correct. When they scored from the second one that was the first time I realised we had Brighton fans above us as they started going nuts, throwing things down on the Leeds fans below and flicking the Vs. Someone said they were throwing p**s too which is not on if this was the case! This caused big issues as the Leeds fans reacted, but it took a long while before the Brighton fans were put in their place by the stewards. I still can't understand why the Brighton fans reacted in that way in the first place, because all we had been doing was supporting our team vocally. Brighton fans were very poor in comparison but there again, not many other fans could do what we do!

At this time, I edged my way through the Leeds fans to go and get my banner. On reaching this I found it really damp which was surprising but there again, with the state of the steps earlier maybe it is something more to do with how the ground is situated. With having to go down lots of steps to the exterior of the ground, maybe it retains moisture, but who knows?

I still maintain that despite losing, the fact the ref was very bad and it was to two penalties, that I didn't feel too disappointed. We may still have a long way to go as a team, et cetera, but I have been given hope back again and I don't go automatically expecting us to lose. We can put up a fight and even though in many aspects this was lacking today, we did manage to defend pretty well for a long time in the second half. As we were coming out at the bottom of the steps a Brighton fan responded to my comment about the ref and penalties, but to be honest it was that insignificant I can't even remember what he said, oops! Also, for a newish stadium I think they need to sort out better lighting at the bottom of those steps as it was very dire when there was a large group of people going up them. There was a bit of shouting at the top of the stairs with plenty of stewards there but nothing really untoward happening.

Despite this being a long trip it didn't feel it, probably as I slept a lot of the way there and back. As I rolled into the house at 4.10 a.m., though, I was glad it was a Saturday morning and I didn't need to get up in a couple of hours to go to work! I'd forgotten we had a game at Elland Road this coming Tuesday too, as we face Reading, and then Brentford at home on Saturday. Pontus got injured last night and I hope he got taken off as a precaution. The Brighton player shoved him as they were near the corner flag and he went flying into the hoardings hurting himself. I'm not sure what the Brighton fans said to him but he reacted badly to them, which was unsurprising. We may have to change the team around a little bit, obviously we have lost Phillips but with a few injuries and having another two games this week, we need to pick up the points. The depths of our team strength may not be so great, but we need to utilise some of the other players to ensure we maximise this. See you on Tuesday – LUFC – Marching on Together!

READING – 13 DECEMBER 2016

After struggling to walk all day due to pain at the top of my leg, I was driving to Elland Road when all of a sudden I had an overwhelming urge of exhaustion that made me want to burst into tears. I decided then to stop off at the White Rose Centre, so by the time my daughter and I got to the ground, it was too late to go to the Peacock. We headed straight into the ground instead and as we passed the East Stand saw that someone had parked their car in front of the stand, so we wondered how long that would last. Luckily there wasn't a big queue nor anyone searching bags when we arrived at the turnstiles. All was looking good until someone in front of us tried to go through the turnstile but it stopped working. The fans in front of us tried the other side and we all thought that one had failed too, but then it started working again. The lad who couldn't get in tried another turnstile, only for it to not allow him in due to having 'read' his ticket at the other one. Luckily he spoke to an understanding steward, who hopefully got him in.

I got to the top of the steps just before the teams came out. It was a damp and miserable night but it didn't feel too cold at that point. It also meant that it affected the quality of the photos I take, unfortunately. The team today was Green, Bartley, Jansson, Taylor, Vieira, Roofe, Sacko, Dallas, Wood, Doukara and Ayling. Subs were Bridcutt (returning from injury) for Wood (went off injured tight hamstring), Mowatt for Roofe and Grimes for Dallas. Attendance was 21,242 with approximately 200 Reading fans.

Leeds started off on the attack before Reading had a good chance, but we defended well to prevent them having a shot. There were some strong tackles going in from Reading and Charlie Taylor was on the receiving end of a few of them. Luckily for us he got up again, but when I think of our players getting booked early doors last week, Reading got away with it surprisingly with no

Reading H 13.12.16 Radrizzani appears at Elland Road

bookings. Bartley had been the hero of the moment as we headed on the attack. As Sacko beat his man and crossed the ball low into the penalty area, as it came to Wood I knew it was going into the net. 1–0 and that felt good, as I thought Reading would be a threat. Not long after that, though, Wood went down injured and he ended up being subbed. As he went into the dugout I'm hoping it was more of a precaution. As it was, it gave Bridcutt the opportunity to come back into the side, having been out since near the start of the season if I remember correctly. I wondered how he would get on coming back into the side after so long out, but there was no need to worry. The rain, although light, had been relentless and Bridcutt's pristine kit showed this up. I wondered why the South Stand started cheering all the passes between the Reading back four but they were taking the mick out of their players. It actually reminded me of how we used to play when we weren't very good. We continuously passed it across and back without ever venturing over the halfway line. Well, maybe a little bit! The thing with Reading was they looked as if they could be dangerous, and I personally wasn't underestimating them. They did have a chance just before half-time but it didn't go anywhere. We had flapped a couple of times in defence but then settled into the game.

After half-time we had another good chance, as Sacko's cross went across the penalty area which Doukara failed to connect with. Green had to make a good save from Reading and there was always a fear that they would get an equaliser, which despite their lots of possession hadn't materialised into too much trouble on our goal. At 80 minutes, it felt like the game was dragging

Reading H 13.12.16

and I had to rest on the back of my seat. Luckily for me, the Leeds fans came to my rescue by upping the ante and taking my mind off things. By singing and getting behind the team it was good to join in the singing, and before I knew it the end of the game drew nigh. Just as injury time was upon us, Charlie Taylor want past the Reading defence and was brought down in the penalty area. With Wood being off the pitch it was Doukara who stepped up to take the penalty and duly scored. That took the pressure off the last couple of minutes, which enabled us to enjoy the remaining minutes without worrying they would equalise. As it was, Reading could have had a goal at the death but we managed to clear it to keep a clean sheet.

It was good to get the three points too and there was a great atmosphere at the end of the game. Although I won't say anything at the moment, it is hard not to join in with 'Leeds are going up'! With our second home game in a week this Saturday against Brentford, another three points will do for me! Fingers crossed so see you there! LUFC – Marching on Together!

BRENTFORD – 17 DECEMBER 2016

I would like to take this opportunity to wish everyone, whether a friend, family or acquaintance, a very Merry Christmas and a Happy New Year. There are many people I know who are battling their own illness or who have lost someone close to them recently. I hope that you get through things in the best way you can under the circumstances and wish you well.

Brentford H 17.12.16

It was a lovely sunny day as we set off for our last home game before Christmas. I had to call at the ticket office to pick up my tickets for the Kids Christmas Party on Tuesday before heading to the Peacock. I was surprised to see the turnstiles still shut at 2.00 p.m., as it's not something I normally take any notice of. I assume it's to save costs but when I think back, if you didn't get into the Kop by 12.30 p.m. you had no chance of getting up to the back when it was standing on the terraces. Those were the days! Once in the Peacock, someone asked if I'd seen Tex – a lad from America who was over – so I went to get his photo along with some other fans.

We got in to the ground about 10 minutes before kick-off and I got the usual photos beforehand. The team today was Green, Bartley, Ayling, Jansson, Taylor, Phillips, Vieira, Dallas, Roofe, Sacko and Doukara. Subs were Berardi for Taylor (who went straight down the tunnel, something to do with his Achilles), Bridcutt for Phillips and Antonsson for Doukara. Attendance was 25,134 with approximately 200 Brentford fans.

The first half didn't have a lot to talk about from our point of view, and if Brentford would have taken their chances then they could have had a few goals. We were making silly mistakes and winning the ball then giving it away again. Out of the mouths of babes: when singing Pontus Jansson's magic – I changed the wording to 'he heads the football back'. Laura said, if he gets a brick thrown at him, how come he heads a football back! Oops, caught out there, lol! We had a

Brentford H 17.12.16

long shot from the left-hand side which I think was meant to be a cross. Their goalie caught it so I asked if that was our first shot on target. The lad next to me laughed and said that I couldn't have that as a chance on goal! Well, it was a case of taking anything from my point of view! We were very lucky not to go a goal down as Brentford put the ball into our net but the linesman put his flag up for offside. That could have been very costly and it was about the third time they'd managed to come down the right-hand side with ease. At least we went into the break on equal terms.

121

Just as I got back to my seat I found out that my granddaughter Laura had spilt her hot chocolate, so I ended up missing the first part of the second half. As we went downstairs, though, I bumped into Trampas, who I hadn't seen for ages and we had a chat as he played Laura some tunes on his penny whistle. He always used to take this everywhere playing Leeds tunes and had everyone joining in, so it was good to catch up with him. The second half started off with the same play as the first, and although we kept trying we were struggling to get a momentum together. I think Brentford would have been happy with a draw, and the longer the game went on the more it looked like heading that way. The fans had been quite restless for a lot of the game but as we came close with a couple of chances from Ayling this changed. The closer it got to the end of the game, the more the fans started to make some noise as the players, despite everything, weren't giving up. I suddenly got a bit of hope as we won a corner. My daughter grabbed hold of my granddaughter as she just had a feeling too, as we took a short corner (not something I like). As the ball came across for Bartley to head into the net all the Leeds fans went wild! The celebrations that followed were absolutely amazing and the rest of the game was immediately forgotten. To be part of this is something to savour and shows what could happen if we carry on in this same vein. The last few minutes passed in a blur but I was still expecting a couple of minutes more when the ref blew for time. Thanks ref for not prolonging this.

Thank you Leeds United, for the very nice Christmas present for us all and another welcome three points. We have just got to keep getting as many points as possible, so time will tell what happens. The Christmas and New Year period are always a challenging time but fingers crossed we can keep going. See you at Preston – LUFC – Marching on Together!

PRESTON – 26 DECEMBER 2016

After all the Christmas celebrations over the last couple of days, it was back to normality today with our trip to Preston North End. With Simon Grayson our ex-manager there it wasn't going to be an easy game. We stopped off in Leyland for our pub stop, where I took an interest in the history of it, before heading back to the coach. Someone passing by on the road beeped their horn, and as I turned round saw the driver going mad and giving us the Vs! With our backs to him the only thing visible from behind us was my Leeds bag, which he obviously took offence to. He also has serious issues if he can take offence at four women walking down the street with a couple of blokes. All we did was laugh at him, and I'm sure his boss would have been proud of him (not) as the van was emblazoned with M. Hindle all over it! Not a good advertisement I'm afraid! As we reached the coach I waited outside it with Julie as I was going to take a photo of fans wearing their Christmas jumpers. Suddenly a police car came past the coach and Julie waved at them. As I turned around I said they were obviously coming to look at what we were doing, as they turned round at the mini roundabout to come back. We both waved back at them as they went on their way but it was nice to see them being civil with us.

Preston A 26.12.16

We arrived at the ground in good time, but instead of parking up outside the away end as usual, we went past and parked up by the park. This meant a long walk back to the ground, which wasn't an issue for us despite the length of it, but it wasn't good for our disabled fans. By the time we got into the ground it was approximately half an hour to kick-off. I was going to find my seat when I was shouted at by Gill and Darren. They had received as presents for Christmas all three of my books, *Follow Me and Leeds United*, *Once a Leeds fan, always a Leeds fan* and the co-authored book *The Good, The Bad and The Ugly of Leeds United*. I was happy to oblige by signing all of them and look forward to receiving feedback after they have read them.

The team today was Green, Berardi, Bartley, Jansson, Ayling, Phillips, Roofe, Sacko, Doukara, Dallas and Bridcutt. Subs were Hernandez for Sacko, Wood for Doukara and Antonsson for Roofe. Attendance was 21,255 with approximately 5,700 Leeds fans, which was another fantastic turnout from us!

The game started off pretty even for the first 15 minutes, before out of the blue we scored our first goal. We had a free-kick as the ball was heading towards the goal from Jansson; Roofe made sure and put the ball into the net from close range. Wow, I wasn't expecting that, to be honest. After Preston came back strongly to try and equalise, we increased our lead six minutes later with our second goal scored by Sacko. Wild celebrations from the Leeds fans ensued with the fact we'd scored two goals in quick succession away from home. It also felt very surreal but that was possibly to do with the fact that I was only four rows from the top of the stand. Our jubilations took a knock a few minutes later as Preston pulled one back. They then put pressure on us to try and get an equaliser before Doukara ran at their defence. He took a shot at the goal and the ball somehow found itself over the line when it looked like the goalie had saved it, giving us a third goal! Going into half-time 3–1 in the lead away from home was frankly unbelievable, as I can't remember the last time this happened recently. It was something to relish, though, and long may it continue.

At the start of the second half, though, Preston came out looking to get back into the game. I said that they weren't going to give up without a fight and it was up to us to make sure we stopped them putting up a fight. Green made a fantastic save to deny them a second goal though, and that was probably a crucial save. Monk made an early substitution bringing on Hernandez who was back from injury in place of Sacko. It took a while for us to get a grip on the second half, though. Preston then made a double substitution with the second one being Jermaine Beckford, famous for scoring for Leeds against man u on 3 January in the FA Cup. I was quite surprised at the standing ovation he got from the Leeds fans as he was now opposing us. Then I thought it was the psychological impact the chanting from our fans would have on him as I said he wasn't allowed to touch the ball. In fact, whatever impact it did have on him he lasted for the grand sum of five minutes on the pitch. He went up for a ball along with Bartley and Ayling and they were all determined to get the ball. The next minute they were all rolling about on the floor, so I thought there was a head injury. All of a sudden there was a red card issued, but we couldn't make out what was happening. I hadn't thought there had been anything in the heading of the ball that warranted a sending off. It was only afterwards that TV replays showed Beckford had kicked out at Bartley whilst they were on the ground and caught him in the face. Sorry Beckford, but that was out of order and you deserved your sending off.

We made two late subs when we brought on Wood and five minutes later Antonsson. It was great that we didn't settle to just see the game out, and after another great attack when the ball was passed to Hernandez he hit it low to get our fourth goal of the game! That was the icing on the cake as we all celebrated and watched as many of the Preston fans emptied the stands. At the end of the game, after the players came to clap our fans, someone behind me asked who was down in the penalty area at the far end which we'd been defending. All of a sudden we realised it was Bartley, who then got to his feet. He, amongst others, had put their bodies on the line today as they fought for the shirt. This is something that had been missing for a long while and great credit to Monk for restoring this back into our players. Hopefully the ones who took a knock today will be fit for Thursday when we head to Aston Villa.

I couldn't believe that at 5.10 p.m. we were still stuck at the top of the stand, as getting out was a nightmare as no one seemed to be moving. Coupled with that was a 15-minute walk back to the coaches, but as I was walking with others we had a good chat so it didn't seem that long. The

Preston A 26.12.16

journey back to Leeds wasn't bad either as I managed to sleep most of the way. That was a great Christmas present for all us Leeds fans today, and for me quite unexpected. I thought we would possibly draw, but the good thing is I don't go to games any more expecting us to lose! Long may this continue as we look forward to our last game in 2016 on 29 December. With all the changing of dates for games on Sky TV, I had got myself totally confused as to what date we are playing on and have now had to change three other arrangements I'd made for Thursday. I will be heading to the game, although we will be going straight to the ground. With a later set-off time it means our pub stop will be in Billy's bar. See you there, and I'm looking forward to a good ending to 2016 as a Leeds United fan! LUFC – Marching on Together!

ASTON VILLA – 29 DECEMBER 2016

After having only played Villa at home at the beginning of December, it felt weird already travelling to the return fixture. Villa Park is a ground I have visited many times before with many memories for the wrong reasons, although some good ones. My first visit in the early seventies had no issues in the 0–0 League Cup draw, until we were stuck in traffic after the game and the coach got attacked. I was there when Glasgow Rangers played a friendly and started off in the Holte End, before climbing the wall to get into the Doug Ellis stand after rioting meant the game was called off after half-time. We played Norwich City there in an FA Cup replay where again I was in the Holte End, but this had a great ending when Clarke scored a hat-trick in our 5–2 win, if I remember right. The ground has improved massively since my first visit there with the open end gone many years ago.

We set off later than usual, which meant we were going straight to the ground. On arrival at 6.00 p.m. we didn't want to go and queue up as it was freezing, so we headed to the Witton pub. There was a sign saying away fans only so we went in there, having to pay £2 each to get in. Villa fans were at the front of the pub with a marquee and we had a marquee at the back of the pub. It was nice to be able to keep warm and we were glad of the opportunity to be welcomed at an away ground. As we set off to go to the ground just after seven there was a minibus across the road, which we realised was the Shropshire Whites. I got a great welcome from them singing my name out of the windows which was really funny, but thank you! The last time I visited Villa Park, our seats were on the front row behind the goal, but this time we were down the side. We had sold all our tickets for this game very quickly and there was still a high demand for fans wanting tickets. Due to Sky TV once again, the game had been changed and it was only last week that I realised I had triple-booked things for the same night! One of these days I will learn to check things properly. One thing that was very disappointing was the stewards refusing to let Leeds fans take their banners in with them. Why on earth they do this is beyond me, because what harm do they do apart from show where our fans are from. It makes a mockery of things, especially when Villa fans had a few banners hung over the front of the stand to our right! Luckily for me I had my blanket with me!

The team today was Green, Ayling, Jansson, Cooper, Phillips, Bridcutt, Berardi, Doukara, Dallas, Sacko and Roofe. Subs were Hernandez for Dallas, Wood for Roofe and Vieira for Bridcutt. Attendance was 37,078 with approximately 3,000 Leeds fans. I'd forgotten that McCormack played for Villa now as he came on later as a sub.

From the start we were put under immense pressure from Villa, who came out looking to get back at us for beating them at Elland Road. Rob Green made a couple of important saves as we struggled to get any momentum going. After the initial 20 minutes, we seemed to settle down and started to have a few attacks. The Villa fans, who had been noisy for the first 20 minutes, were very quiet for most of the game whilst the Leeds fans were in full voice. The thing that really disappointed me was some Villa fans to the right of us spending more time calling a young Leeds girl a slag than supporting their team. Very classy, I don't think so. This is one thing that really winds me up having suffered the same things at the hands of lads in the seventies, but is something I thought had been left behind in that era. Shame on you, because she has been to more football games that many of you have had hot dinners and at least supports her team!

Going into the half-time break at 0–0 felt quite a decent result, to be honest. I know many of us would have taken a draw at that point. Today I had many of our fans asking for their photos taking and was happy to oblige. I also managed to catch up with a couple of Halifax Whites and the mascot for Leeds today. It had been really good to catch up with Carol at the start of the game, who has been through some gruelling treatment recently and it was good to see her back! Having been given Pontus's shirt recently it was good to see that had made her really happy, and was well deserved.

The second half really belonged to Leeds as we came out a different team. I think in the first half we had stood off them a bit but we kept trying to play some decent football and worked hard with our passing. Villa still were not going to give up, though, and there was plenty of end to end football. We got a corner and as the ball went across into the middle of the box, Pontus rose to head the ball which beat the goalie, creeping over the line right in front of us. The lad next to me ended up with coke all over him which had come from the Leeds fans above us. Great celebrations once again from us, and we could have had two very shortly after with a nearly identical move which saw Pontus hit the crossbar! Now that would have been the icing on the cake. As it was, Villa were still coming at us and not giving up, which probably was a good advert for football for the neutral fan. Today was the first time I really felt nervous as I so wanted us not to lose this lead. There was still 15-20 minutes left though, which seemed to drag. As it was, Villa were offered a lifeline with the awarding of a penalty, damn! To be honest, the first thing I saw was their players rushing to the ref and nearly knocking him over. I was surprised they got away without any bookings, though, cos they actually manhandled him. With that and the howling of the Villa fans, he went over to talk to the linesman and gave the penalty. He was actually nearer to the incident and it didn't look like he was going to give anything. I will have to see it for myself but was disappointed that we didn't

manage to keep the ball out of the net. Well, to be honest I was hoping that he would miss the target, which he didn't, sadly.

That set up a frenetic last six minutes or so and although Villa could have got another, so could we. The most glaring one was when Sacko beat his man again down the side where we were, and all he had to do was pass the ball into the centre for Chris Wood to stick in the net. Sacko also hit the crossbar which was so unlucky. Unfortunately, neither happened so the game ended in a 1–1 draw, which was probably a fair result. It was quite disappointing not to have got a win but when I think back to not so far in the distant past, it just shows how things have changed for us. At one time we'd have been glad to get a point.

As we came out of the ground I was surprised to see the Villa fans all being let out past us, especially after the vitriol they had shown to our fans. This passed without incident though, but one Villa fan was stood at the side chanting away and trying to get a reaction in my opinion. It took ages to find our coach and I was beginning to think I would just jump on any one to get back to Leeds, but luckily I found it at the back of the car park. As one of the last fans got back on the coach he said it had been very hairy getting back to the coaches, but if something did kick off, I was certainly glad it wasn't anywhere near me! The only downside was not leaving the ground until 11.10 p.m., when we had been kept on Witton Road for over an hour after the end of the game. I couldn't believe with all the police presence that they didn't get us on our way as soon as possible. Once we did get on our way, though, we were back in Leeds just after 1.00 p.m. with another half an hour to get home.

Finally, I would like to wish everyone a very prosperous, happy and healthy New Year, and for those of you who have been ill, get well soon. See you at the Rotherham game – LUFC – Marching on Together!

CHAPTER 7 – JANUARY 2017

ROTHERHAM – 2 JANUARY 2017

Happy New Year everyone, and today I'm looking forward to a change in fortunes for Leeds United this year.

Yesterday Leeds put the 'sold out' notices up again, apart from the part of the West Stand allocated to the Rotherham fans with approximately 500 of them coming to the game. Although it was 12.30 p.m. the car windscreen was still iced over, with the temperatures not much above freezing. It was going to be a cold day but the sun was shining, although dazzling, so at least it felt good to be heading to Elland Road.

The team today was Green, Bartley, Ayling, Jansson, Berardi, Hernandez, Roofe, Doukara, Sacko, Wood and Bridcutt. Subs were Vieira for Sacko, Dallas for Doukara and Antonsson for Wood. Attendance was 33,397.

It was good to see a full Elland Road again, but unfortunately for the fans the first half didn't live up to what was expected of the team. It was always going to be a tough one despite Rotherham being at the bottom of the League, and to be honest they could have been one up very early on. We have Green to thank for that because he made a fantastic double save to deny them. Our chances were very limited in the first half as we struggled to get any momentum going. Rotherham, on the other hand, were putting us under pressure but luckily for us didn't actually put the ball into the net, which could have changed the game. I felt that we needed to get a corner to give us a chance of getting near the goal. My daughter couldn't get over the fact that Roofe was wearing a long-sleeved top and gloves but wore his socks at half-mast. She really wanted to go and pull them up! The atmosphere wasn't great in the first half with only sporadic chanting and singing, but one moment had everyone as quiet as church mice. Luckily that didn't last long, though.

At the start of the second half Vieira came on to replace Sacko, who had a slight knock. Within a couple of minutes we were in the lead, as our first attack won us a corner. As the ball was swung into the middle Bartley jumped up, never taking his eyes off the ball, and headed it into the net. Unfortunately, as he ran off with the rest of the team to celebrate Jansson had to receive treatment for a while, but luckily for us he got up again despite a paramedic being in attendance too. This start was just what we needed as the second half belonged to Leeds. We scored a second fantastic goal when Wood got the ball with his back to the net and their defender on his back. He somehow turned and hit a powerful shot into the net with a cracker of a goal. That took the pressure off us somewhat and then when Roofe had a fantastic run down the East Stand side he passed the ball into the middle for Wood to get his second goal of the game and Leeds a three-goal lead. Once the fans saw the response from Leeds at the start of the second half they responded well, getting behind the team. It was even better after celebrating the three goals. We were unlucky when Berardi had a shot that hit the post and a free-kick from Hernandez also hitting the post. To be honest, I missed them hitting the post but as the lad in front of me is taller I have to try and see around his head! The one thing I haven't seen in a long while was the entire Leeds dugout stood up when we had an attack!

That was a welcome start to the New Year with another three points, that keeps us in the playoff spots. Although there is a long way to go, the run this last couple of weeks, giving us 10 points out of a possible 12, is the best I can remember for a long time. Before our next League game versus Derby, which has been changed to a Friday night because of Sky, we have Cambridge United in the FA Cup, also changed because of BT. Why they can't be on a Saturday or Sunday is beyond me and whilst I appreciate fans around the world want to see us play, I wish they would keep the travelling support in mind. A good Cup run would be great and all Leeds should do is go out and enjoy the moment and see where we end up in both the League and Cup. Winning breeds winning, and the best form of defence is attack! See you at Cambridge – LUFC – Marching on Together!

CAMBRIDGE – 9 JANUARY 2017

This one was going to be a late set-off, and I was lucky that I was being picked up by a friend who was doing the driving. We had a good journey there and were able to park up opposite the ground, albeit with a 10-minute walk away. With it being close to kick-off the early arrivals had cadged the spaces nearer to the main road.

As we approached the ground we were shown where to go to our stand and found ourselves in the middle of loads of Leeds fans all arriving together. We had to walk down a path with a field next to it the length of the side stand, to get to the other end where we were based. As there had been heavy rain all day and there was lots of mud and puddles about we stuck to the path. Despite getting there late we got in before the start, hung my flag up and then told we could sit anywhere! After seeing Phil Cresswell outside I found Mouse, who I hadn't seen in years, and it was good to see him, although only for a couple of minutes.

The team today was Silvestri, Denton, Mowatt, Antonsson, Cooper, Jansson, Dallas, Grimes, Berardi, Doukara and Phillips. Subs were Coyle for Berardi, Roofe for Doukara and Bartley for Cooper. Attendance was 7,973 with 1,414 Leeds fans.

The game kicked off at a fast pace but after an initial burst from Leeds, we found we were on the back foot. For some reason we could not get our passes to work as Cambridge attacked us time and time again. I thought that it would take us about 20 minutes to settle into the game, but the longer it went on you knew we were struggling. We had no shape and didn't look like we had any tactics, being all over the place. The referee looked like he was going to book everyone in our team after booking three in quick succession. He was very lenient with Cambridge in comparison, letting many things go and he kept the book in his pocket for them. His decision making was terrible and after he gave Cambridge a free-kick, we ended up going a goal down after 25 minutes. I'm not sure if the ball hit someone on the way into the penalty area and changed direction, as I was expecting it to be on the same side as we were stood. Somehow it went across to the other side of the goal where their man beat our defence to put a low ball into the goal via the near post, with Silvestri rooted to the spot. Oh dear, this didn't bode well, especially as after their goal they could have had a couple more. The Leeds fans got quieter and quieter as the reality of another game against a lower League club looked to be heading in the wrong direction. The ball wasn't running for us either, but we were struggling with the pace of Cambridge and kept getting turned inside out.

The lads next to me said they were going to go to the pub at the opposite side of the ground and watch it there at half-time. I did say it could be a game of two halves again, though. I must mention Bob from the White Rose Branch, who had got out of his sick bed to attend the game. After doing a fantastic 60 years of following Leeds United he reckons this may be his last season of attending games. Whether it is or it isn't, that is a brilliant record and well done to him. It puts the team to shame when fans are making this sort of commitment for little reward. Just before half-time, Mowatt got hold of the ball and sent a shot soaring into their penalty area which their goalie had to tip over the bar. Mowatt had been one of the few trying in the first half. I knew what was coming when the players were booed off the pitch at half-time again, although I didn't boo. One player we didn't expect to see again in the second half was Doukara who had been atrocious, either giving the ball away or every time he got the ball he couldn't control it. We were all glad that the whistle blew to end our first half misery. We also started feeling the cold at that time.

We walked to the opposite end of the stand to where we came in and found it relatively empty at that end, and those queuing for the tea bar were pleasantly surprised at how quick they got served. Whilst we were stood there, first aiders came past with a Leeds lad who had blood trickling down his face from a head wound. As everything had been so quiet we couldn't understand what had happened but just hoped the lad would be okay. Someone said they would sub Mowatt in the second half, and I said no way as he was one of the few actually doing something. My judgement was spot-on in the second half as he was involved in one build-up and scored our second.

As we went back to the stand, the only sub made was Coyle for Berardi. At the start of this half we immediately got stuck in and started to apply some pressure, and it didn't take long before a great cross from Mowatt was headed into the net by Dallas to give us some hope. It was a quick turnaround again as a corner was headed on by Jansson and Mowatt put this into the net to put us into the lead! We suddenly found out feet, and even more so when Roofe came on and we were then able to see the end of the game out comfortably as Cambridge probably ran out of steam too. It meant that Leeds were drawn away against Wimbledon or Sutton in the next round, which means the Forest game at home on 28 January will be changed.

We were very lucky that once we hit the A1 that there was very little traffic on the road, so we had a good run home singing to music all the way back. I thought getting up at 6.30 a.m. was early but my friend had to be up at 5.30 a.m. – the things we do for Leeds!

We head into Friday's game at home to Derby, another televised game, without the services of Jansson who got booked in the first half. This means he is one game off activating a clause for a new contract, although I've no idea of the ins and outs of it. It's also looking like being extremely cold, so wrap up warm everyone and safe travels. See you there – LUFC – Marching on Together!

DERBY – 13 JANUARY 2017

Setting off to work in snow this morning, it was good to hear that it wouldn't last and the game wouldn't be affected tonight. Although it was to be cold, that was good to know. We didn't arrive at the ground until after 7.00 p.m. and I'd thought we wouldn't get to the Peacock, but managed 15 minutes there. On our way into the ground there were plenty of fans in good spirits, singing and shouting.

Today was to be the first official visit of our new co-owner, Andrea Radrizzani. One of the few times he has attended Elland Road was against Newcastle when I took a photo of him in the West Stand, which made it very popular with the media. Although I hadn't realised I'd caught him on camera it was a bit of kudos for me!

The team today was Green, Berardi, Ayling, Bartley, Coyle, Vieira, Bridcutt, Roofe, Doukara, Wood and Hernandez. Subs used were Dallas for Roofe and Mowatt for Hernandez. Attendance was 25,546 with an approximate 1,000 or so from Derby.

Listening to BBC Radio Leeds on the way there, Noel Whelan read out texts from some fans and one had said they thought we'd lose with the line up we'd got. I just thought maybe not, we'll see. The one thing I would say I was surprised at was that Doukara kept his place from Cambridge, as he had a very poor game there. He does have some strength and pace which is probably what was behind Monk's thoughts. The game kicked off at a very fast pace, though, as Leeds began on the attack. We came near a few times as we won corner after corner but couldn't put the ball into the net. The closest was a driving shot from Bridcutt that their goalie put over the top for another corner. Derby were limited to the ball for long spells as we kept driving forward, looking for the breakthrough. There was a great atmosphere around the ground too. Suddenly Derby had an attack, and if I remember right it was on the 29th minute. My initial thoughts were – I hope we don't suddenly concede a goal now, after all the attacking play we had been having. Lucky for us, Green was able to make the save to prevent them before we went on the attack once again.

Just before half-time we had another corner, and this time luck was with us when Wood headed the ball into the net to send the Elland Road crowd into raptures! What a time to get a goal and another cracker from Wood – his 17th of the season according to BBC Radio Leeds. Derby went straight down the other end from kick-off, only for Green to make a great save to prevent them from equalising right before the whistle went. We went in at half-time deservedly in the lead, plus that first 30 minutes had flown by. I had said a few weeks previously that the best form of defence is attack, so I'm glad that Monk listened to me, lol! At the start of the second half, Derby came out fighting and put us under pressure for a while. They had made a double substitution and the blond-haired lad Will Hughes had run rings around us at Derby a few years ago. Suddenly the ball was in the back of the Leeds net which had us all looking at each other; were we grateful to see that it had been disallowed! Thank goodness, as it looked like the subs had paid off. All of a sudden, with the Leeds fans getting right behind the team with a great WACCOE, we started to attack Derby once more. The Leeds crowd were absolutely fantastic with the best atmosphere we have had at Elland Road for a long time. The scarf-waving was really getting going with WACCOE but it was also the whole ground joining in. It was after Derby had a man sent off for a second bookable offence (I didn't realise it was Bradley Johnson, who used to play for Leeds, until afterwards) that some of the Derby players were wilting as the Leeds fans became the twelfth man. It's a long time since we have had a fortress Elland Road and getting that intimidating atmosphere back, although tonight came very close to that. Although Derby had a couple of chances to get back into the game, the night belonged to Leeds United and our fantastic fans. Getting the three points put us up to third in the table, our highest position in the League for I don't know how long. I cannot honestly remember the last time we played out of our skins for 80 minutes of a game and not just for half a game either. The fact it was televised will show just what is happening at Leeds, and the fact is the sleeping giant has awakened and we are on our way back. There may still be a long way to go but whatever happens, we can savour the win and the atmosphere from tonight and be thankful that there is no place like home and Elland Road is the place to be! I was quite surprised to get home after the game to find our street still covered in ice and snow. At least it didn't affect the rest of the journey.

Next Saturday sees the late kick-off at Barnsley at teatime. I've no idea what time we are setting off but we are probably going straight there. Last time they opened the Leisure Centre for the Leeds fans to go for a drink, so it is possible they will do the same again. Before that I have a small operation to go through on Monday evening, so I may look a little battered the next time I see everyone. Nothing too serious, I have been told, and once it is out that should be it. I've waited over a year for this so I'm actually looking forward to getting it over. See you at Barnsley – LUFC – Marching on Together!

BARNSLEY – 21 JANUARY 2017

It was touch and go at one stage this week as to whether I would make the game today. After my surgery on Monday evening I went in to work for a meeting late on Tuesday afternoon, and went back in on Wednesday. I only lasted an hour on the latter day before being sent back home due to being sick. Later that day my face and eye began to swell, and by Thursday I looked like someone had lamped me one. Luckily, with antibiotics both orally and eye drops, the swelling and infection had eased by today so at least I made it. Although feeling weary just before I got to Billy's bar, I soon began to look forward to the game. A Yorkshire derby was always going to be a tough one but I said we should go out and play our best, enjoy ourselves and let others worry about us. Barnsley isn't a good ground for us results wise, though, but I was hopeful we could carry on where we left off last week.

As I was taking photos in Billy's bar, I asked to take one of Terry Yorath and some fans who were sat with him. One said did I want to be in the photo too, and I said no, he's probably had plenty taken with me, and then as I got a reaction said I didn't mean anything by that! (We'd seen him at the recent kid's Christmas party.) One lad then said are you the one who takes photos all the time and puts them on WACCOE and are you Heidi? After saying yes, he said he looks through about 200 photos (I know I get carried away sometimes!). Another one said yes, everyone always waits for you to post your photos, and I said I know, sometimes I'm falling asleep but have to keep waking up to make sure they get posted. It was nice to know that my photos are looked out for!

We left Leeds at 4.00 p.m. and had to go past the Barnsley turnoff to the next one and come back up north to the junction, as apparently there was more space to hold the coaches there. As we headed off to the ground in a police escort we thought it wouldn't take us long but thought it too late to go to the Metrodome, where there was a bar put on for Leeds fans. As it was, the escort took that long to get to the ground that it was already 5.10 p.m. and we hadn't even parked. Everyone then got off the coach along with hundreds of fans at the same time and headed down to the ground. There was only a small entrance for everyone to get through to the turnstiles, but we managed to get through them relatively quickly. Once inside the ground, though, we got under the stand and tried edging along with everyone else. Those who had been in earlier were already watching approximately five lads sat across the metal pipes that went across from one side to another. It also looked like there had been a smoke bomb let off. Once we came out of the toilets there had been a yellow one let off and it stunk foul. We tried walking to the entrances with everyone else and that was when things took a turn for the worse. More and more fans came behind us and it was getting very scary and we were all starting to get crushed. It was bad enough for us but as one lad told us after, he had his son with him and it got so increasingly bad that he nearly had to put him on his shoulders. Because of this I decided to go up the first entrance into the ground to get out of the crush. It's a long time since I've experienced anything like this, and there were plenty of stewards as we came into the ground who should have held some fans back to prevent this in my opinion.

All of a sudden, this lad behind me shouted he's got a broken collarbone for crying out loud, or words to that effect. I looked round to see him trying to protect his son, but then he started arguing with the lad at the side of him and nearly came to blows. Unfortunately, in a crowd it is hard not to get carried along with everyone and I don't think anyone was intentionally doing anything. I then decided to go behind them to try and protect the back of them but the chap still wasn't going to let things drop, and I really thought they were going to come to blows. The poor young lad kept trying to calm his dad down and eventually they went their separate ways. As I was stood at the top of the stairs deciding which way to go, I recognised Josh Warrington in front of me. I then went down to the front after trying to get a photo of him but I'm sure I wobbled the camera. It was then I realised that the front two rows of seats were cordoned off and there was room to put my flag up after all. I put it up right behind the goal then went to find my seat, which was in the upper tier. I ended up right above the entrance but it didn't feel safe at all. Probably because everyone was crammed in together but also the bar wasn't very high, and I thought it would only take a push for you to go head over heels over the top.

The team today was unchanged with Green, Bartley, Ayling, Coyle, Berardi, Roofe, Wood, Hernandez, Vieira, Doukara and Bridcutt. Subs were O'Kane for Vieira and Dallas for Bridcutt. Attendance was 17,817 with 5,241 Leeds fans.

It didn't take long for Barnsley to come out with all guns blazing as they were at us from the go. After approximately 15 minutes we managed to get to the other end and won a corner. I said we should make this count, as we hadn't got near there very much up until then. As I zoomed my camera in someone said something and I said I'd managed to get the ball going into the net last week. With that, I took a picture as Wood put the ball into the net to put us into the lead, only to wobble so much that all I got was a blurred photo! Oh dear, but it was good to get the goal against the run of play. As we scored, the Barnsley fans to the left of us either chased some of our fans out of the corner or were just trying to get to the Leeds fans. There was also something kicking off at the left-hand side of the far end too. I'm not sure if it was anything to do with any Leeds fans or not, though. We managed to get a few corners as we played on the attack but gradually Barnsley got back into the game, courtesy of the number of free-kicks given by the ref. Honestly, the amount that were being given was so over the top as the Barnsley players would take a slight knock and fall over when they should have been able to stay on their feet. It was after another free-kick just before half-time that they managed to equalise as we didn't clear the ball. It was a timely goal for them just before half-time. They nearly got a second just before the whistle blew, too.

At half-time I went downstairs on to the concourse, which was more sparsely populated than before the game, and went to some different toilets further under the stand. As I was in a cubicle I heard someone shout, 'If you are going to use the ladies loos then for crying out loud shut the

bloody door!' I knew straight away that the lads were using the ladies loos once again. Why they can't use the gents, I have no idea why. I realised then that the whole toilets looked a complete mess with water all over the floor. It was only as I was coming out that I found the reason why, as a woman told me the first toilet had been kicked over. I knew then that this was not caused by any female fan but by the lads using the ladies. I had heard that some fans damage the toilets on occasions, but for the life of me I cannot understand why? We are better than this and do not need any wanton destruction of anything. It has taken us years to get away from that reputation but some fans seem to be hell-bent on getting that part back again. One thing I do not agree with is damaging anything, and if any of us females would have seen it happening then I am sure we would have tried to stop it, our fans or not!

As I was going back into the stand some young lads asked for their photos taking. I then went to the front of the stand to get photos of all the flags and took a few of fans who shouted me. At the start of the second half Leeds carried on where they left off, as Barnsley once again took the game to them. With only a few minutes on the clock Barnsley took the lead, as they looked to attack us with ease. A group of lads next to us tried to get some clapping going at around 50 minutes and were chanting 'There is only one Mark' (together with his last name). Unfortunately, as I joined in there was only this small group who were doing it. I realised this was for a Leeds lad who had died recently.

I said we needed to change things but we didn't, and before we knew it the ref once again gave them a free-kick in a dangerous position. Straight from the free-kick the ball beat the wall and as Green stretched out he was nowhere near tall enough to get anywhere near the ball! Damn and double drat! The one thing I have noticed is that with Green's lack of height he needs some protection in the box. Why we don't have a man on either post is beyond me, to be honest. With Billy Bremner and Paul Reaney saving loads of chances over the years, it makes sense to me that we do this for set-pieces or corners. After leading 1–0, all of a sudden we were losing 3–1 within 10 minutes of the restart. We were under the cosh and with another Barnsley attack there must have been at least six Leeds players at the back not marking anyone. We were at sixes and sevens all over the place and I was screaming at Monk to change things. He eventually did after a few moments, but I reckon we should have changed whatever formation we were using straight away in the second half as it wasn't working. Some players were trying but half of the time we were second best. We did manage to pull a goal back when Chris Wood was attacking the goal in front of us. As the defender tried to clear it the ball hit his hand, and the ref had no hesitation in pointing to the spot. He only had a word with the Barnsley player, though, when I thought it should have been an automatic booking for it. Chris Wood put the ball into the net, sending the keeper the wrong way, to give us hope that we could at least get a draw out of the game. We had a couple of chances, but the longer the game went on the less likely it was looking that we would get an equaliser. When five minutes extra time was put up I thought we stood a chance, but as the minutes ticked away I got a feeling that there was no chance that we would score and unfortunately I was right. It was a very disappointing result for us but apart from all the free-kicks Barnsley got, which helped them immensely, they probably deserved the victory.

As the game finished one of the Leeds players took his shirt off and gave it to someone stood at the front of the stand, which was a nice gesture. Plenty of fans clapped them as they went off the pitch, though, despite their disappointment with the score. As it was a very fine drizzle I wrapped my scarf around my head to prevent my wound getting wet, which worked very well. After an hour of being escorted away from the ground we eventually found ourselves back on the M1, but at the junction we had to turn around at earlier. It was quicker getting back to Leeds from there than it had been to get from the ground. As I left the coach to go back to my car, Terry Yorath passed me and said something as I said goodbye! I then picked my daughter Dani up, who had travelled with the White Rose Branch, and we headed for home.

We have our rearranged game with Forest on Wednesday, before next Sunday heading to Sutton for the next round of the FA Cup. It will be an early morning call as it is a 2.00 p.m. kick-off but at least I can sleep on the coach. I was talking to someone in the ground who went to Sutton the last time we played them. He said that all of a sudden in the ground the Leeds fans got attacked by a load of Chelsea, Tottenham and West Ham fans (I think that's who he said) and they had a right battle on their hands. The next thing a load of fans with blue and white scarves jumped over the fence to join the Leeds fans, and when asked who they were they said they were Millwall. They hated Cockneys and had come to help the Leeds fans against them! You learn something every day!

Before I finish, it is looking more and more likely that I will be unable to go to the Birmingham game due to the change of the game due to Sky TV. To say I am mad is an understatement, as I never expected this! If so, then unfortunately I won't be there to take any photos or do my blog for those of you around the world who look forward to them. Okay, luckily at least you can see the game for yourselves, but for me personally, to change it from a Saturday to a Friday night is something I hate!

See you on Wednesday – LUFC – Marching on Together!

NOTTINGHAM FOREST – 25 JANUARY 2017

It was going to be a very cold evening, with the temperature dropping as we headed to Elland Road. My granddaughter Hannah was very excited to be going to the game and her highlight would be seeing Lucas the Kop Cat, hopefully! I'm very proud that in a couple of weeks Hannah will be having 12 inches of her hair cut off to help children with cancer, raising money for Candlelighters at the same time. A very worthwhile cause!

After a quick visit to the Peacock to meet friends, and also to keep warm, we headed into the ground approximately 15 minutes to kick-off. To say we were expecting a 22,000+ crowd, it felt very quiet outside Elland Road. One thing I've noticed is that many fans arrive late to evening

Forest H 25.1.17

games, so that was maybe why. In the ground and with 10 minutes to kick-off, most of the stands were still quite empty but that soon changed.

The team was Green, Bartley, Jansson, Berardi, Ayling, Hernandez, O'Kane, Roofe, Dallas, Wood and Bridcutt. Subs were Doukara for Dallas, Vieira for O'Kane and Mowatt for Hernandez. Attendance was 24,838 with approximately 500 Forest fans.

As the game kicked off we had a chance very early on, before Forest took the game by the scruff of the neck for a while. They brought out a great save from Green to prevent them taking an early lead. Not long after that we had an attack, and when the ball came to Chris Wood in the penalty area I thought he'd kicked it wide. Just as I realised it had actually gone into the net I had to calm down quick as it was disallowed for offside. As Forest had been in the game a lot until then it would have been against the run of play, not that I'd have grumbled! We were very lucky when Berardi was on hand to head the ball away from our goal, though, in what could have been a great chance for Forest. We struggled at times to get any momentum going but the half actually went past very quickly and I wasn't wishing it to end as I have many times in the past.

At half-time we had been discussing the game so far, and I said it hadn't been brilliant. Keith then said it will be a better second half after Garry Monk's half-time talk! Well, Keith, you got that spot-on as we came out a different side to what went into the dressing room. We won a corner at our end and I was looking forward to catching the action with my camera, only for Wood to score and I ended up with loads of heads on a photo as everyone in front of me jumped up! All of a sudden, after never being able to do anything from a corner, we had perhaps turned a corner and were getting on the scoresheet from them! Now that is something us Leeds fans have been waiting a long time for. When Monk made his first substitution I was surprised to see Dallas come off the pitch to be replaced by Doukara. My first thoughts were that I supposed Garry knew what he was doing, as he seems to be quite astute in some of the decisions he makes. Well Garry, you did know what you were doing as Leeds won two corners on the bounce. From the second one the ball went back out to Doukara who was on the edge of the penalty area, and he volleyed the ball hard and it flew into the top corner of the goal to our right! Wow, that was a gem and it has been said it took approximately eight seconds to hit the back of the net after the ball left his foot!

That was it then, as Elland Road exploded and it looked like it was going to be our night. It is such a shame that the best move of the game in my eyes didn't end up with a second goal for Wood. As we raced out of defence with some beautiful one-touch football, I know it involved Ayling but can't remember who else now. The ball was crossed into the box only for Wood to not get to the ball to bang it straight into the net. It was a fantastic move and deserved to have a goal at the end of the action but whatever happens, it was good to see the actual movement and football involved in the move.

Forest H 25.1.17 Alex Mowatt last Leeds game

There were a lot of happy fans heading home at the end of the game and Hannah said it had been awesome! She also loves Billy's statue like me and thinks he was wonderful! I've trained her right! It is nice to have the next generation of fans enjoying the game, but also seeing the quality in the second goal. I'm lucky, having followed Leeds for such a long time I have seen fantastic goals from the likes of Billy Bremner, Peter Lorimer and Tony Yeboah to name a few. For some of our fans who have been starved of success over the years, this may have been their first time of witnessing a goal like the one Doukara scored.

We didn't hang about long at the end of the game as we wanted to get home. By the time we got to our car, though, the majority of cars in the area had already gone. It was -2° when we got home so it was nice to get in to the warmth. Hopefully by the time we play Sutton away on Sunday, it will have got a bit warmer. I am one of the lucky fans to have got a ticket and will be heading down south with the Fullerton Park Branch for the 2.00 p.m. kick-off. Fingers crossed we can get a win, as the team will probably be changed as per Cambridge. Winning breeds winning Leeds, so here's to a good game of football! See you there LUFC – Marching on Together!

SUTTON, FA CUP 4TH ROUND – 29 JANUARY 2017

Before I start my blog today, I am skipping to the end product. Disgraceful Leeds United, treating both the fans and the FA Cup with such disrespect. Fourteen away games fans had to attend to get a ticket for today, with some people up at 3.30 a.m. and others arriving here the day before showing commitment, which is something the team didn't do. Consensus amongst the fans at the game was that the fans should be reimbursed by the club! The one thing I will say is that Sutton thoroughly deserved their win, as they were the better team on the day and up for it. I can accept us losing but what I cannot accept is the way we lost it! Shame on you Leeds!

After only having four hours' sleep due to waiting for a phone call from the out of hours doctor that didn't come, I was up at 5.00 a.m. and sat in McDonalds at Elland Road very bleary-eyed by 6.00 a.m. At least I knew I could sleep on the coach. After talking to my friend Sue for a while we both fell asleep, and woke up with a start as we pulled into Watford Gap for a short stop. After that we headed to Epsom for our pub stop, before getting to Sutton in plenty time for the 2.00 p.m. kick-off. It had forecast torrential rain for the start of the game so I asked the home stewards, who were waiting for us as we got off the coach, if I could take my Leeds United golf umbrella in with me. They were very helpful and went to ask the question from a head steward, and said there would be no issues with me taking it into the ground.

There was a nice feel about the place as we headed into the non-League ground. Although my friends Carole and Margaret were at the game Leeds played there in 1970, it was my first visit to the ground as I didn't start going away regularly until 1971. Plenty of Leeds fans had brought their flags with them and they were all hung around the side of the pitch. It was a tight enclosed ground with a 3G turf, but I'm sure it wouldn't be as bad as the old plastic pitches that we used to visit, for example Oldham. That was always a bad ground for us to visit!

Sutton A FA Cup 3rd Rnd 29.1.17

Sutton A FA Cup 3rd Rnd 29.1.17

Sutton A FA Cup 3rd Rnd 29.1.17

The team today was a big disappointment, as Monk made *10 changes*. As a traditionalist, this was a disgrace with not taking the FA Cup seriously, as we should have been putting out a strong team in my opinion. In my mind, winning breeds winning and we would be lucky to win this one. The team was Silvestri, Cooper, Denton, Phillips, Coyle, McKay, Whitehouse, Dallas, Antonsson, Doukara and Grimes. Subs were Sacko for Dallas, Wilks for Doukara and Roofe for Whitehouse. Attendance was 4,997 with approximately 774 from Leeds.

The rain started right on kick-off but luckily, although fine, wasn't the torrential rain that we'd been expecting. As someone pointed out to me, as I was stood right behind the net, if I put my brolly up then those behind me wouldn't be able to see. If the rain got that bad I was going to move to the side, but I didn't need to put my brolly up in the end.

Sutton were up for it from the word go, with Ian Baird, an ex-Leeds player, being their coach. There were only a few minutes on the clock when we thought Sutton had taken the lead as the ball hit the back of the net in front of us. As Sutton fans were celebrating the linesman had his flag up for offside, which was apparently only millimetres out. If we thought that would gee Leeds up, we were sadly mistaken. We couldn't get into the game, as the team struggled to get any momentum going and showed they weren't used to playing together. We did manage to get a shot in from Dallas, which the goalie saved, but I think that was our only chance in the first half. Sutton had a

Sutton A FA Cup 3rd Rnd 29.1.17

few saves from Silvestri that prevented them from taking an early lead. We couldn't believe it at half-time when Sutton watered the plastic pitch!

If we thought the first half was bad, the second half didn't get any better. We had one tame shot on goal from Grimes but we still didn't look like we could score in a month of Sundays! To make matters worse, Sutton were bearing down on our goal and I thought, what on earth is Silvestri doing at the edge of the box as he collided with Coyle. As Coyle scrambled to get up he inadvertently brought a Sutton player down to give away a penalty. The ball was sent into the bottom right corner, whilst Silvestri was sent the wrong way. To make matters worse, Cooper was sent off for a second bookable offence, reducing us to 10 men not far from the end of the game. Stats at the end of the game said we had over 60% possession! We all looked at each other and said no way did we do that, or put it this way, we didn't do anything with that possession!

There were a lot of angry Leeds fans at the end. The amount of effort put into getting there by fans only to be treated to a reserve game rather than an FA Cup game was rightly condemned by everyone around me. As I said, we can take losing but it is the manner of losing that we cannot take. There was no pride for the shirt or effort to look like we wanted to win the game. As Leeds sold Alex Mowatt on Friday, and with many fans saying we didn't need him, well, today showed that he should not have gone! He was head and shoulders above the majority on the pitch today and I am positive he will go on to have a good career at Barnsley and good luck to him.

We have now got a difficult week, with two more away games at Blackburn and Huddersfield facing us. We have only two days of the transfer window left but I have no idea how this will pan out. After today's disastrous result it is important we get something out of these two games. Forgive me if I don't feel as positive as some who say the play-offs are guaranteed. I don't see it that way, as there is a long way to go, and I only hope we don't self-destruct in the meantime. Obviously, time will tell and I take each game as it comes. Admittedly there will be a lot of players coming back in to the team and I'm hoping they can pick up where they left it. The only good thing about the defeat is the fact that Ipswich will be a Saturday game – TV, keep away from us, we don't want any more changes! See you at Blackburn – LUFC – Marching on Together!

CHAPTER 8 – FEBRUARY 2017

BLACKBURN – 1 FEBRUARY 2017

I picked up Gary and his daughter Ella before heading to junction 25, where the coach was picking us up. This worked really well, and although we had some queuing we only had to do a diversion nearer Blackburn. We pulled into the services for the police escort but didn't get off the coach, as the police said that when they were going if you weren't on the coach, we would be left behind! Most of the others on the coach had been in the services and got back on at the last minute. As it was, we waited for approximately 15 minutes as there was only our coach and the South Kirkby one there before we pulled off in the escort, and we were one of the first coaches to arrive there by about 6.30 p.m.

As soon as we got off the coach there were a few police officers there, who immediately started talking to Sue and I. They were very nice and it was good to have a nice welcome on arrival. The other good thing was that Blackburn had put on a fan zone behind the away end, which was another good move. I had received a tweet from one of my Selby members on the way to the game who asked me if I remembered one of the Sweeting lads from Old Goole getting stuck in the turnstiles at Blackburn in the eighties. I couldn't remember, but I got the chance to ask one of them as he was in the fan zone. What a coincidence! He said yes, it was his younger brother who ended up coming back out of the turnstile as he couldn't get through, so they had to open the door to let him in!

I went in early to go and find a good position for my flag, and got one right behind the goal. It was good to see the flags again from the different areas, including the Bournemouth flag whose owners were stood behind me in the ground.

I decided to go down for a cup of tea and some others who had travelled to Sutton were talking about the day. We all agreed it had been a disgrace for the fans, the FA Cup and for Sutton, who would have relished playing against our better players. We had quite a good conversation with a few more joining in. Unfortunately, a young lad got the brunt of our displeasure when he started to say that this was the best chance of getting promotion, we didn't need the Cup and we should rest the players. Sorry lad, it may be our best chance (I agree on that point), but I will never agree with the fact that the Cup wasn't important as winning breeds winning. It also meant a lot to the fans who travelled there, too. One thing that I couldn't really agree with, though, was the resting of players. I agreed that Pontus would have been one to rest just because he had played the required number of games to sign, and also because he does seem to carry an injury. But it was the fact the lad said that they needed to be kept for the League games and that he played football twice a week and always ached, so how the team felt…My retort was that they are professional footballers, and after seeing how Billy Bremner showed what playing for Leeds is all about, they should have been trying to win both. He said, even if we had no chance of winning the Cup? I said we should never have thrown the towel in like we did, and I never thought we would stoop to those levels. I hadn't intended having a rant but there were quite a few around me in agreement with what I said.

I moved to the side and was waiting to see if Tony was coming in (who will be part of our group arranging the recording of all the old Leeds songs) and saw quite a lot I knew. A couple of fellas to the side of me then asked if I had gone everywhere in the seventies, so we had a good chat about following Leeds. Of course, I used the opportunity to showcase my books before heading into the ground for kick-off. Once in my seat, I realised that probably the reason why we had been welcomed so much by Blackburn was because their attendance looked very poor. I asked someone if the Venkys were still involved in the club and whether there were still protests going on, hence the low crowd? I was told yes, so I think that has had an impact.

The team today was Green, Bartley, Jansson, Berardi, Ayling, O'Kane, Bridcutt, Sacko, Roofe, Dallas and Wood. Subs were Hernandez for Sacko, Doukara for Roofe and Vieira for O'Kane. Attendance was 17,026 with 6,402 Leeds fans. This was also the first away game that our new co-owner, Radrizzani, was in attendance.

We didn't start off too bad but Blackburn had the ball in the net very early on, so I was glad when it was disallowed, for a foul I think. In the first half Blackburn had a lot of the ball and at times seemed to skip around our players with ease. As time wore on we got a free-kick, and as I wondered who our free-kick specialist would be, Wood stepped up to the mark but the shot went wide. The longer the game went on I could see that Blackburn were not going to give up in a hurry. I said, they are not going to lie down and die as it's up to us to make them. For some reason, I kept looking back to the scoreboard to see how many minutes of the half were left, and it was always only a couple of minutes had passed by! The half did seem to go on for a long while but we never tested the goalkeeper. Someone in front of me said that he was so glad that we had rested all our players on Sunday at Sutton! To be honest, it felt like we had lost that momentum and had gone backwards. I felt that the midfield wasn't working as well as it should and that was why Blackburn had plenty of the ball. I also thought that Monk should make an early substitution, which is one thing that he does seem to get right more often than not. It hadn't been a good half, to be frank. The Leeds fans had started off well but it kept going quiet in places, probably due to the lack of things happening on the pitch. With a minute of injury time left I headed down to the front of the stand to get some photos of the Leeds flags on show, before heading downstairs.

At the start of the second half Hernandez came on for Sacko, and although Blackburn still had a lot of the ball we did look better. O'Kane wasn't having the best of games in midfield and he got spoken to by the ref, and when he fouled one of their players shortly after I was quite surprised he didn't get booked. As it was, Pontus ended up in the book again. Doukara came on for Roofe and we changed formation slightly and things looked more positive. Up until the 70th minute, though, we didn't look particularly effective and the Leeds fans were starting to get restless, with

some even booing them. We did start to up the pressure and the Leeds fans chanted attack, attack, attack, attack, attack. The Leeds players responded immediately, and before we knew it the ball came over to Dallas and he struck the ball into the back of the net to put us into the lead! Relief all around from the Leeds fans, as everyone celebrated. It was only then that I realised the upper tier of the stand was full of Leeds fans too! The game wasn't over by a long shot, though, as Blackburn came back and before we knew it the ball was in the back of our net for them to equalise. The ball was struck from a long way out but as it bounced it looked to fool Green and he couldn't save it. My heart sank then, as that put them back into the game. I went down to the front of the stand just before the end of the game to ensure I could get to my flag. I stood on the steps and a steward was stood behind me. She said that I would be better moving, because if Leeds scored all the fans would come hurtling down the steps. She was the second steward who had been really nice to us and she also must have had a premonition. I moved over to the seats near my flag as Leeds won a corner in the last minute of the game. As the ball came over all I saw was a figure loom out of nowhere with no one near him, and I knew the ball was going into the net for a last-minute goal! Unbelievable scenes followed with fantastic celebrations in the whole stand going nuts. It was only as the rest of the Leeds fans started singing Pontus Jansson's magic hat that I realised it was him that had scored. I just assumed it was Wood! The majority of the game was forgotten in an instant, because getting a last-minute winner was just what was needed.

At the end of the game, Jansson came across to throw his shirt into the crowd to the right of us. It landed on the netting at the front and as some fans were trying to get to it, a steward stopped them, and then got it and handed it to a little boy. I then realised it was Paul and his son Reuben from Halifax as I got photos of them, and I was chuffed to bits for the lad.

The timing of the win couldn't have been better, because it has given us some momentum again and also, with our next game against Huddersfield on Sunday with an early kick-off, that is something we will definitely need. They will be up for it as usual as they try to put one over us. Without our win today I could have seen us struggling, but now I look forward to us hopefully getting a win. At least we have enough points now to forget about relegation this year! Those days do actually seem a long time off, and that shows how far we have come. See you at Huddersfield – LUFC – Marching on Together!

HUDDERSFIELD – 5 FEBRUARY 2017

I didn't set off until 10.30 a.m. today as I was driving to it. As I listened to BBC Radio Leeds on the way in they were saying that lots of fans were already turning up and the roads around the ground were getting busy. I decided to drive the back way in and got to the ground at the same time as three Leeds coaches. When I parked up I had a very good position at the front, but I thought I'd have to wait a while as usual after the game to get out. I don't watch any other football on Sky or TV so I had no idea what to expect today, but I thought whatever happens it would be a tough game. I hoped we could sneak a win but a draw would probably be a good result.

I wasn't going to take my banner with me today, but saw a message on Twitter saying flags would be allowed but there wouldn't be much space to put them up. I did take my bag with me then, which also has copies of my three books in. It was a good job I'd taken them in the end, as I sold one at half-time! It was good when a Town steward prior to the game told me that he enjoyed reading my blog every time too, which is really good to hear!

Leeds had a reduced ticket allocation for this game as the Town singing section, complete with drum (I know one of the lads who does this), had taken over the other side. What I will say is that despite the annoyance of the drum constantly banging away, it has improved their atmosphere by a long way. The one thing I cannot understand is their absolute hatred of us? Until we ended up in the same division, we never knew they existed!

The team today was Green, Berardi, Ayling, Bartley, Jansson, Vieira, Dallas, Doukara, Wood, Hernandez and Bridcutt. Subs were Pedraza for Doukara, Barrow for Dallas and O'Kane for Hernandez. Attendance was 22,400 with 1,958 Leeds fans. As the teams came out I realised it was only 12.00 p.m. and was surprised as I still thought the kick-off was at 12.30 p.m. No wonder there had been lots of fans heading to the ground! I'm sure I'd asked someone recently what the kick-off time was and they'd told me the latter. Never mind, at least I got there in time!

There was no doubt that we would have to come out of the starting blocks straight away today, as we couldn't afford to sit back and let Town come at us. This certainly was the case, but at times we were struggling to contain their players who came nearest to opening the scoring, although we did have a very good chance in the early minutes. We were getting out-muscled and although Bridcutt and Vieira were at times getting out-fought, they did manage to overcome that in the first half and stopped giving the ball away so much. Our passing wasn't as good as it should have been, which put us under more pressure. I also thought that with the amount of fouls on Vieira that were let go by the ref, that certainly had an impact on him, but he never gave up. When one of their players went off injured I hoped that this would upset Town, but unfortunately for us it didn't. Jansson had made a great tackle on the edge of the box only for the ball to go straight to another Town player, which wasn't long after the substitution. The sub then got the ball and put it into the net in front of us to put them into the lead. Damn, damn, damn! I thought the way he ran across the Leeds fans trying to incite them wasn't on either, before he flung himself into the Town fans to the left of us. It wasn't a surprise that they had got a goal, though, but I wasn't sure how we would react. I think that is also the noisiest I have ever heard from the Town fans after they scored, as loads at the left-hand side ran to the front of the stand to goad the Leeds fans.

Earlier, when we got three corners in succession, I knew we had to make the most of them but sadly nothing came of them. We did come close on a couple of occasions, though. I'm not sure how long it was before we got the ball back up to the other end again, but I had high hopes when we got a free-kick on the edge of the box. Once Hernandez put the ball across I thought the ball

was going in all the way, when first Bartley then Wood got on the end of it once again to score! It seemed to take an age before it did, though, and trying to take photos with a jack-in-the-box at the side of me was pretty hard, but I couldn't blame him for celebrating in that way! It did shut the Town fans up though, thank goodness! Berardi made a fantastic tackle in the penalty area to deny them a goal straight after we scored. As half-time approached I was hoping the score would stay that way, but I felt we had got stronger as the half progressed.

As I was going up the steps at half-time I met Jo from Halifax, who was with Raluca from Romania who was here to see Leeds again. I should also give a shout-out to the Leeds fans who had travelled up from Cornwall for the game, having left at 2.30 a.m. to get here for the early kick-off. Well done to all our fans who have travelled great distances to the game, although for once I didn't have far to travel from Halifax. On chatting to some of our fans we all would have accepted a draw at that stage, but still hoped we'd sneak it. It was nice to meet up with Mouse at half-time and show him his photo in my first book!! Thanks for the support! Next time, Huddersfield, please ensure us females don't have to negotiate a flood and get wet feet in the ladies!

The second half kicked off and although the pace wasn't the same as in the first half, we still kept giving the ball away. The referee also must come into this blog because I thought he was horrendous! I am all for keeping the game moving but the amount of times he let fouls go on Leeds then immediately blew as we tried to get the ball back was unbelievable. Booking ours even though they got the ball first and letting Town carry on regardless is not very good in my eyes. Our new boy Alfonso Pedraza was brought on in place of Doukara quite early on, and the first attack he had saw their goalie make a fantastic save. At one point, though, I thought Berardi was having to do more work as although Doukara hadn't been as effective as he might be, he did help him out a lot. Pedraza will have to work on tracking back, although to be fair to him, we have only had him a few days! Our other new boy, Barrow, came on to replace Dallas and when we won the ball in the centre, it should have been passed straight out to the wing to him only for us to see the ball go the other way as we lost it. Hernandez wasn't having a good game to be honest, and I always thought that Monk would replace him at some time, which he did when O'Kane came on. Unfortunately, he didn't make much difference, when I felt he should have come for a few balls and he seemed to stand and watch it instead. I suddenly looked round at the scoreboard to see that 87 minutes were on the clock, which had also passed very quickly. It made me think of the time we scored in the last minute to win there. I wished I'd not looked around to see how much time was left, because right on full-time with Town attacking us at the far end of the pitch, I thought their man was offside as he stuck the ball into the net for Town's winner. The ball had come off another player, but listening to Radio Leeds later they confirmed the ball came off a Leeds player so it wasn't offside. With that, I noticed someone in a black coat charging down the pitch towards the Town players, celebrating. I thought, what the…I didn't think they were allowed to do that? The next thing, I just saw everyone going berserk in the dugout area as all the players ran over to try and stop whatever was going on. It took ages before calm was restored and first Wagner was sent to the stands and then Monk. Monk just went straight down the tunnel instead.

That was a bummer, but I knew then that we were not going to get anything out of the game sadly. It was a disappointing way to end but we will move on. As I've said to others, we need to concentrate on our own performance and just keep getting as many points as we can and see where we end up. On today's performance, Town are the best side we have played this season. Things are very tight in the top six and in this division anyone can beat anyone on their day. As I headed to the car, just as I got to the edge of the car park, a policeman stood there said, 'Don't worry, we will still go up!' It was good to get straight out of the car park too and find myself already at home by 2.30 p.m.!

We have Cardiff at home next week in our first 3.00 p.m. kick-off for a long while. In my opinion that is a traditional time and we should have more kick-offs at that time, instead of everything moved for the cameras. There should be some way around it that lets our fans around the world still see us, and I look forward to the day that travelling fans are thought of when arranging kick-off times. See you next week – LUFC – Marching on Together!

CARDIFF – 11 FEBRUARY 2017

I couldn't believe my eyes when I drew back my curtains this morning, to see a damn magpie sat on my lawn mocking me! I decided to put it to the back of my mind as I tried to work out who we played in our last game as well! When I realised eventually it was Town last week, I thought, out of sight out of mind! It just shows how I forget about things very quickly when I want to!

We didn't arrive at Elland Road until 2.15 p.m. today and Leeds were expecting another 30,000+ crowd with only a small contingent coming from Cardiff. We went to the Peacock for a quick visit, then we headed to Billy's statue as I had arranged to meet Nigel to sign my book. I had met him at Town last week and he'd asked if I could sign the book this week, and I was happy to oblige. As we stopped at Phil Beeton's programme cabin in the Peacock car park, we bumped into Nigel there, which worked out really well.

As it was cold today many fans came onto the terraces right on kick-off, but it was good to see a nearly full ground. The team today was Green, Bartley, Cooper, Berardi, Ayling, Bridcutt, Hernandez, Dallas, Wood, Vieira and Pedraza (making his home debut). Subs were Sacko for Dallas, Roofe for Pedraza and Doukara for Vieira. Attendance was 31,516 with approximately 350 Cardiff fans.

Leeds had plenty of the ball in the first half but it didn't take me long to have that sinking feeling in my stomach. I said that I thought it was going to be a frustrating game today with both Warnock and Sol Bamba returning as the opposition. One thing that caught my attention was the fact that we were passing back to Green all the time, and playing passes across the back four lots of times. As my motto is the best form of defence is attack, I wondered why we were playing so

Cardiff H 11.2.17

deep. Instead of playing to our strengths, for some reason we had reverted to type from earlier in the season. Cardiff themselves weren't very good but they did manage to get a few good runs past Ayling, and whenever they crossed the ball we had to battle to keep them out, which we did really well. We have Berardi to thank for getting in the way of a great shot from Bartley, which unfortunately was heading straight into our goal! We didn't really put Cardiff under pressure despite all the possession we had, and although we did have some good passing, never really looked like scoring. The ref went off to a round of boos at half-time as he started making some bad decisions, one when we had got a throw-in. He kept moving us back and then gave the throw-in to Cardiff, with Bridcutt getting booked for protesting.

We started the second half on the attack and I was hoping for better things this half. We weren't able to take advantage of this, though. Cardiff won a free-kick, and when the ball went into our penalty area there were two Cardiff players with no one marking them, and one of them put the ball into the net to give them the lead. To be honest, either of them was going to score. It really felt that we weren't going to get back into the game as any shot we had at goal was very tame. Bartley saved one on the line at the other end before they got a second goal and it felt like normal service had resumed at Elland Road, sadly. Bridcutt then got himself sent off for a second bookable offence, in what I thought was a harsh decision. Looking at it from the Kop, the Cardiff lad ran

164

past Bridcutt but then left his leg out behind him which he had no need to do. Bridcutt caught this leg, hence the second booking. That was it then, game over and disappointment that despite all the possession, we didn't really play well. I felt really sorry for the fans who had travelled miles to get here for this game, including 400 from Norway and some from Cornwall.

We have to pick ourselves up as we have another home game on Tuesday against Bristol City. It is imperative that we sort ourselves out, play to our strengths and not change our style to suit Bristol. See you on Tuesday – LUFC – Marching on Together!

BRISTOL CITY – 14 FEBRUARY 2017

Luckily for me I was heading to Leeds from Halifax, so my car journey took approximately 20 minutes. Fans coming from the opposite direction had to endure snail-paced traffic due to an incident westbound on the M62, which backed up along the M621 and the ring road in Leeds. I was due to meet one of the lads from the now defunct Selby Branch of the Leeds United Supporters' Club in the Peacock who'd got caught up in the traffic. Luckily, he got there for a catch-up. For any other Selby members (I saw two more today too), there is hopefully going to be a meet-up after the Sheffield Wednesday game as it's an early kick-off. It was nice to have a chat with some of our Irish fans before the game, too.

The team was Green, Bartley, Jansson, Ayling, Berardi, Vieira, O'Kane, Roofe, Sacko, Wood and Hernandez. Subs were Barrow for Roofe, Phillips for O'Kane and Doukara for Hernandez. Attendance was 22,402 with approximately 300 Bristol fans.

It was important that we stepped up our game today, as things hadn't been going our way just recently. It was also the first game for a long time that we'd been turned around to attack the Kop in the first half. We started off well and had a couple of chances, but they weren't on target. The first time we had a stray pass was in the 7th minute, which was a big improvement. We were lucky that Green was in great form tonight because he was called on to make an early save to keep Bristol out. Leeds then had a couple of shots on target that their goalie had to save. Jansson got the ball to the left of the penalty area and beat their man to put a cross in, which raised our game. At that moment, I wasn't sure whether we would get a goal, but I didn't have long to find out. Leeds were given a free-kick, which was taken so quickly by Hernandez that he took everyone by surprise apart from Chris Wood. He reacted well to put the ball into the net, whilst I kept waiting for the ref to disallow it as it had been taken before the ref was ready. For once luck was on our side as the goal was given. I had my camera poised to take a photo and all I had to do was press the button, but for some reason I was so mesmerised I 'dropped' the camera to watch the action and missed it! Oh well, all that matters is that we scored! Luckily at half-time we went in with a goal lead, despite Bristol putting us under pressure just before the whistle blew. As I took a photo downstairs, the plaque for the Revie Stand in the Kop looked decidedly shabby and I look forward to the day that we can get it refurbished!

Bristol City H 14.2.17

The game changed again in our favour when we attacked the South Stand. Hernandez shot, only for the ball to be deflected wide of the goalie to put a bit of light between us and Bristol! That came out of the blue so soon after half-time but gave us a cushion. Bristol never gave up, though, and for me the man of the match was Green as he made some great saves to keep them out. I felt quite calm, though, because even though Bristol kept attacking we were playing better and had a lot of possession ourselves. At one point all the South Stand and the team shouted for a penalty, which was for a handball incident. I couldn't see it at the time but have seen a video shared online, and it was a unanimous shout for a blatant handball. Chris Wood also got past their goalie but couldn't get the final shot in to give us another goal. I'll give Bristol their due, because they still kept attacking us and on a different day I'm sure they'd have got something out of the game. Having seen them get something out of the game in the last few minutes down at Ashton Gate, I wouldn't just accept the score with minutes still to play. One shot that Green saved from them was unbelievable, as I have no idea how he managed to keep that one out of the net! We were put under pressure continuously during the five minutes of injury time as they won a few corners. With more or less the final kick of the game Bristol pulled one back, as Green was unlucky not to keep a clean sheet.

For once luck was on our side and I am grateful for the three points to get us back on a winning streak. I will take each game as it comes and just look forward to us keeping going and getting as many points as we can. I will then see where we are later in the season, but fingers crossed we will still be amongst the top six! We head to Ipswich on Saturday, and the only good thing to come out of the Sutton game is the fact we don't have to travel there midweek! See you there – LUFC – Marching on Together!

IPSWICH TOWN – 18 FEBRUARY 2017

As I set off from home it felt eerily quiet even though it was 7.15 a.m., but at least the sun was rising making it light. It gave me a positive feeling to the day as I stopped the car at the side of the road to take a couple of photos.

Our pub stop today was in Bury St Edmunds where we have stopped for many years. I love the pub here as they have retained so much of the old features, which I think are great. As well as our coach, there were both the Vine Branch and South Kirkby Branch in there too. As we all arrived at similar times the pub had a challenge on to get everyone served, although we were lucky as we didn't have to wait too long. Having already decided what I wanted to eat, I had to change my choice as it wasn't on their menu. Both Sue and I decided on jacket potatoes only to find they'd none left! If that's all we had to worry about then it's not an issue, never mind. It was nice to find fans coming up asking about my blog and having their photos taken. It was also nice to have a chat with a couple of our younger fans from the South Kirkby Branch. Then another one came to chat

Ipswich A 18.2.17

who I'd taken a picture of in an incident in the home stand at Blackpool, which was really scary for him and some others.

We got a policeman on a motorbike giving us a personal escort to the services, and then approximately 12 coaches were escorted to the ground. We got into the ground by 2.30 p.m. despite all the coaches arriving at once, and again it was nice to have stewards saying hello and smiling. I put my banner up and had a chat with a few fans including Vaughan, his son George and friend Jack who go everywhere. I'd also been reminiscing with Steve about our visits to Paris and Amsterdam, and also the realisation that they were 42 and 41 years ago respectively. Where has the time gone, as we remember them like yesterday but can't remember who we played last week, lol! I was also talking to a couple from Bournemouth who hadn't brought their banner in, due to problems they'd had before the game. They'd been in a pub near the station which was packed. There were loads of queues for the toilets upstairs as the toilets downstairs were locked. Why? To then send men into the ladies was a disgrace. The lad complained, as there were women and children having to use them with men going in as well! Where's the logic in that? One of the staff took exception to his remarks and reported him to the police, who then did a check on him. He said he was sick and tired of it as they take one look at him and decide he's a troublemaker! Having been following Leeds for nearly the same time as me, why do they automatically think he wants to cause trouble?

The team today was Green, Ayling, Bartley, Jansson, Berardi, Vieira, O'Kane, Dallas, Wood, Sacko and Hernandez. Subs were Bridcutt for Vieira, Barrow for Sacko and Doukara for Wood. Attendance was 18,745 with 2,113 Leeds fans. I was also surprised to see that Leeds were without a mascot again today. Why, I'll never understand, with the amount of youngsters we had at the game? It's possible someone couldn't make it at the last minute, but are we limited to one mascot away from home?

It's always a bogey ground for us here and Sue had said beforehand that she didn't know how it would go, whilst she was talking to an Ipswich fan in Bury St Edmunds. I wasn't sure either, and sometimes prefer to see how we are playing in one sense before making a judgement. One of my memories from Ipswich was about 15 of us getting ambushed in the Sporting Farmer near the ground, which I've mentioned in my book *Follow Me and Leeds United*. Some things you never forget! I also remember Bobby Robson being the only one to get tickets for a group of us Leeds fans at the opening of the ground in Eindhoven, when it had sold out. Thanks Bobby.

We had a couple of attacks, but before we knew it we were a goal down in the 8th minute. The ease with which Ipswich went through the middle of our team into the penalty area to score didn't look good at all. Passes had already been going astray but we really made it look so easy for them. Once again, up against it with our backs against the wall. We struggled to make any impact at all, to be honest, and whatever tactics we were using made us look very dire. Ipswich were the ones who came close to scoring and always looked dangerous. The Leeds fans kept getting behind

Ipswich A 18.2.17

the team with a 10-minute rendition of 'We all love Leeds', and must have put some motivation into the team. As half-time approached I was talking to the lad next to me, saying that I was sure Monk would make some changes early on in the second half. We also felt there must be something more going on, due to the fact that the whole team collectively seemed to have lost their way. I still stand by my stance that we should have gone out to win at Sutton, as winning breeds winning and nothing I have seen since that day will convince me otherwise. Almost in slow motion we got the ball into the penalty area and everyone seemed to stop as the ball came to Dallas, and he had time to put the ball into the net. Phew, just in the nick of time to give us a fighting chance.

I was comparing cameras with Paul at half-time as he explained an action on his. I have to admit that despite all the thousands of photos I have taken, unfortunately I still haven't read the instructions yet, oops!

The second half saw Bridcutt come on for Vieira, but unfortunately the game carried on in the same vein as the first. Our passing collectively was very poor and once again we have Green to thank for a great save to stop Ipswich getting a winner. Also, it's a good job Bartley was on the line to head one out that eventually came back in for Green to catch. Our other substitutions didn't have an impact but we managed to get to the final whistle to keep it a draw and get a point. The only shot on target for us was our goal, which showed how poor we were, unfortunately. The only good thing to come out of it was that we didn't lose and got the point away from home, so we will have to take that as a positive. I was very surprised to hear Monk saying the pitch had been very poor in his talk after the game. That wasn't anything the fans around me had seen, sorry!

It had been a good day out with good company, despite the 90 minutes at the game. It was also nice to be back home in Halifax by 9.30 p.m. as I remember the days when we used to take at least five hours to travel back to Leeds along the winding roads. As I reached King Cross there were police everywhere and a car on its roof, so I'm glad I missed that!

I know many fans are worried that we are going to drop out of the play-off spots and at times it looks as if that could happen. I still maintain we should just go out and get as many points as we can and play to our strengths. We seem to have gone to playing very deep and having a lot of passing from side to side before giving the ball away. I don't know what the answer is, but there will not be any easy games as anyone can beat anyone in this division. Next week sees the visit of Sheffield Wednesday to Leeds in an early kick-off in one of those crucial games, so we have to raise our game at Elland Road. It also looks as if we have got another 30,000+ crowd, so let's make it a fortress Elland Road and sing our hearts out for the lads. I'm hoping to meet up with my old Selby Branch lads after the game too. So fingers crossed for next week, see you there – LUFC – Marching on Together.

SHEFFIELD WEDNESDAY – 25 FEBRUARY 2017

As we headed to Elland Road to see the game in front of a 35,000+ crowd, I was still adamant that we should play to our strengths, enjoy the game and let Wednesday do the worrying. That should enable us to get something out of it! After a visit to the Peacock I met a chap who knew me from years ago and asked if I remembered Rowan from Hull, who he used to travel with. I did remember Rowan from the eighties and fantastic support from the chap who had been going to Leeds games since 1948! We got into the ground just in time for the early kick-off of 12.30 p.m., and also another televised game.

The team was Green, Bartley, Ayling, Jansson, Berardi, Hernandez, Sacko, O'Kane, Doukara, Wood and Bridcutt. Subs were Roofe for Sacko, Vieira for O'Kane and Dallas for Hernandez. Attendance was 35,093 with approximately 2,800 Wednesday fans.

We were turned around for the second time in recent games so that we were attacking the Kop in the first half. Leeds had possession for a lot of the opening minutes without getting a clear chance on goal, before Wednesday came close. It would have been Sod's Law for them to score, but instead it was Leeds who took the lead shortly afterwards. Berardi crossed the ball from in front of the West Stand and again it was in slow motion as the ball evaded everyone and came through to Chris Wood all on his own. He proceeded to put the ball into the net with us looking to see whether it had been disallowed for offside! Nothing appeared on the horizon, so with our first shot on target we had scored! We had another chance shortly after, but Sacko kept the ball longer than he should have, which meant we lost the chance.

SheffieldWednesday H 25.2.17

Sheffield Wednesday H 25.2.17

Half-time came with us still in the lead. There came a message over the tannoy to say that the half-time penalty taker was to be a lad on his stag do. It turned out to be the young lad from the Bolton game who was filmed when we were relegated. To say that he is now getting married, it shows how much Leeds fans have had to endure the dark times over numerous years since our demise. It also says a lot about the loyalty and commitment shown from our fans during those times as we are still here! With fans like the Cornwall lads from Falmouth, who were setting off at approximately 2.00 a.m. to get to Elland Road in time for today's game, I appreciate what our fans do to follow our team.

The second half saw Leeds really under the cosh for most of it. Wednesday were out to get an equaliser, along with the help of a very poor ref. They only had to fall down when tackled and they got free-kick after free-kick. Admittedly some were indeed free-kicks, but to hand out bookings left, right and centre was over the top. When one of theirs went down I'd said that I thought the ref would have sussed his diving out by now, so it was with great satisfaction to see his next dive get him booked for his efforts. Admittedly we all thought it was Bartley who had been booked, as we all collectively groaned at the thought of him being suspended. It was a relief to see the decision go the other way for once. When Wednesday were awarded a penalty, our hopes were down to Green in goal. Well, he certainly pulled off a fantastic save to prevent Rhodes from scoring from the penalty spot, to send the Leeds fans into raptures. Wave after wave of attacks still came our way and the players battled and defended for all they were worth to prevent them from getting an equaliser. We didn't have many chances of going forwards and at times we were our own worst enemies. The number of times we nearly got caught out at the back by passing the ball amongst ourselves had us with our hearts in our mouths. Bad passing contributed to that too, but if you looked at the hard-fought game where they were putting their bodies on the line, well, we can't have it all! I kept shouting that the best form of defence is attack and we had to stop inviting them to attack us by playing deep! This had my granddaughter Hannah in stitches, due to the fact I was telling the players directly what they should be doing. The second half seemed to drag, with 20 minutes to go and then into injury time. We took some pressure off us in the second half when Monk used the subs, but until the final whistle went there was no way you could relax, as Wednesday always looked dangerous.

In one of our rare attacks Wood carried on with the offside flag up, putting the ball into the net, only to get booked for his effort! The Leeds crowd should also get a mention as we never stopped getting behind the lads and being the twelfth man on the pitch. It was great to see the ref blow his whistle to end the game and know we had got the three points in the bag. We had also done the double over Wednesday after winning at their place too. At the end of the day, it wasn't pretty from our point of view, but all that counts is we got the points in the end.

As we walked out of the ground the rain started again but it wasn't too bad. It was nice to bump into Derek from Ireland, who I had met at our pre-season friendly last year in Dublin. As we carried on to the car, it was very frustrating personally to know that I wasn't going to be able to go to our next game at Birmingham. Due to this being changed by Sky to Friday next week instead of Saturday, changing the day is causing me to miss it. Apologies in advance to everyone who reads my blogs, but if anyone wants to write a bit about the game and/or send me their photos, I will still post them. Otherwise my blog will be missing next week.

As we are already at the end of February, there aren't that many games left and many more will be tough. We have another away game at Fulham, before two home games in succession against QPR and Brighton. We just need to keep playing, getting as many points as we can, before seeing where we are in a few weeks. Time will dictate whether we get to the play-offs, which are a lottery, but if we can get there, who knows what will happen. See you soon – LUFC – Marching on Together!

Sheffield Wednesday H 25.2.17

CHAPTER 9 – MARCH 2017

BIRMINGHAM – 3 MARCH 2017

Thank you to David Watson from Linthwaite and Bobby Joyce for these reports. Thanks for the photos Bobby! A big thank you to Vaughan Milliken for his photos too, as they are greatly appreciated.

So, in the absence of Heidi Haigh who couldn't make it to the game (sorry you missed the game, Heidi) here's a shortened version of a short review of the Birmingham away game. Apologies for the complete lack of photographs too. I can't compete with you on that one Heidi. I left Huddersfield at 2.15 p.m., a half day off work, home to feed the cat before picking up two mates in Huddersfield City Centre. I also picked up in Sale off the M60, which meant we had a full car. We were feeling confident that we would at least get a draw. Journey to the ground was very good (less so in the return journey – more of that later) and we were parked up just after 5.00 p.m. Luckily, I'd had the foresight to pre-book a parking spot with the app Just Park, which was very handy being a five-minute walk to the ground.

We were turned away at the first pub and were recommended The Cricketer's Arms. What a great pub. Good atmosphere and the bar staff were extremely efficient, meaning a round for four people was despatched expeditiously and at a reasonable price. We left the pub at 7.35 p.m. and we're taking our seats as the game started.

The game: I thought we were poor first half; the only thing of note was Wood's clever lob. He is on fire at the moment. Second half was much better and when Kalvin Phillips came on we looked more threatening. Wood's second goal was a well-worked team goal, but the third by Pedraza was sublime.

The journey home was a nightmare, with both the M6 and M60 closed meaning we got back to Huddersfield at 2.30 a.m. Despite having a full car, there was room for the three points. I must give a special mention to Dave, Tom and Spence who were great company, and it would be good to travel with you guys again. On to Fulham; nothing excites me in life nowadays but I am so looking forward to Fulham. It would be good to win, but a draw would not be a disaster. Brighton lost today so second place may not be out of reach. See you all at Fulham on Tuesday.

– **David Watson**

When I visit St Andrews now – as I have done frequently since 1981 following Leeds – I think of the versatile Bryon Stevenson who starred for both clubs. He died too young. The match last night was shown on Sky Sports so I need not go on about the game, apart from saying three points was a bonus! I am a Midlander so although I have visited Elland Road many times, I tend to catch up with the team at my local grounds. In 1981, I was behind the manager's bench and personally collected my first Leeds autograph from my hero and then manager Sniffer Clarke. I met him years later with Jonesy (that squad was a family) and many others of the Super Leeds gang over time. Bryon came onto the scene as we were fading but he was a decent honest player, and it was strange seeing him play against us for Brum the following year. Worthington, who came to Leeds in a swap deal, did a sterling job but came too late to stop relegation. 'Elvis' is reported to be struggling with his memory nowadays, but when I met him three years ago he could not stop talking about Super Leeds and how he'd watch them whenever he could at night games when he was at Huddersfield! Shez had his time here too, including that painful 1987 playoff match and later the League Cup semi (shame about the Final – a dreadful day at Wembley, although I got Eddie's and Paul Hart's autograph outside the Towers). In 2004, I saw a downcast Norman Hunter leaving the ground (radio work) after the 4–1 defeat and the oncoming spectacular fall of Leeds, but is our time coming again? It would be remiss of me not to mention the late Gary Sprake, who played for both clubs and who paid a heavy price for breaking ranks. A top goalkeeper (we all make mistakes). I tend to watch away games in a 'neutral' part of the ground as I got fed up years ago being treated as a hooligan. Nevertheless, Leeds fans are always close by and I can't describe the swell of pride I get whenever I look at the massed ranks of the noisy, loyal, barmy Yorkshire Army – this is what makes Leeds special and supported from far and wide – MOT. Match Summary: Wood was the difference. Leeds were sloppy in their passing but held together by Pontus and Green at the back. Phillips made a big impact on coming on as sub. Blues will just wonder what happened!

– **Bobby Joyce**

FULHAM – 7 MARCH 2017

I had a later set-off time today but at least it meant that I could get to the game, and thanks once again to fans who helped me achieve that. We arrived at the game not long before kick-off, but got there in time. Getting through the turnstiles was an achievement in itself whilst carrying my bag and coat. Whoever designed those turnstiles wants shooting, as they were so narrow I was sure I was going to get stuck in them, but luckily by coming out backwards I ended up inside the ground. I bypassed the bag searches and the sniffer dogs with no issues or checks and got into the stand ready for the teams to come out. Although there was a 'neutral' part in the stand we were in, this had been taken over by the Leeds support so there were at least 7,200 Leeds fans there, as we had sold out our own allocation. There were also another 1,500 watching the live beam back of the game at Elland Road in both the Pavilion and Billy's bar, which were also sell outs. Fantastic support again from the Leeds fans, with a Norwegian and Irish contingent there also.

Ayling was missing due to his partner giving birth to a baby girl, and congratulations to both of them, and Wood was injured. Because of this we had Taylor coming back in at left-back for his first game after his Achilles injury, with Berardi switching to right-back. The team was Green, Taylor, Berardi, Jansson, Bartley, Phillips, Pedraza, Bridcutt, Roofe, Sacko and Doukara. Subs were

Barrow for Sacko, Dallas for Pedraza and Vieira for Roofe. Attendance was 22,239 with 7,200 Leeds fans. Phillips was sent off in the 90th minute for a second bookable offence, although with the retaliation of their man he should have gone too! At the time, I thought Phillips shouldn't have been sent off and the more I see his tackle on TV, in my opinion he got the ball!

The Leeds fans were in good voice and it was good to see the whole stand being Leeds. Within five minutes Leeds were ahead after a free-kick was put into their net with an own goal and one of our first attacks. I nearly got seasick then and had to hold on to the seat in front of me, as the entire stand started to shake with the celebrating Leeds fans. Omg, I didn't like that at all and kept expecting the stand to collapse under us. Also, trying to take any photos with the shaking stand was nigh impossible. Up until then Fulham had been pretty quiet, but that was soon to change as within 10 minutes they were constantly attacking us. With Leeds fans chanting 'If Berardi scores we're in the Thames', some may have been sweating when his shot at goal was on target and saved easily by their goalie! Although a lot of the attacking was coming down Berardi's side, he defended well, often putting his body on the line. We couldn't get the ball off Fulham and again Bridcutt's passing was very poor, often giving the ball away to their players. We were under the cosh for most of the first half and then they hit the crossbar (I was told after that the ball had gone over the line but the ref didn't see it) so we got away with that decision. To be honest, it all happened that fast when it came down onto the goal line, that I couldn't tell one way or the other at the time. It was good to get to half-time without them equalising, though.

Getting to the toilets and back under the stand at half-time was absolutely manic, with everyone in high spirits. As I made my way back to the section stairs I needed to go up, I heard a lot of banging and then four stewards came past giving an escort to a green dustbin. I noticed then that lads were lining up at the fence to dive into the Leeds fans seemingly having fun. There was also a Leeds fan at the other side of the fence and up a tree, who obviously hadn't got into the ground. He got his Leeds flag out, started waving it and then had the Leeds fans singing about him being up a tree! It was funny, though, as I laughed to myself on my way back to my seat just in time for the second half.

At the start of the second half we had a bit of a respite, with us doing some attacking before Fulham got the game by the scruff of the neck again, meaning we had to defend. As we were playing deep I don't think that helped, but at times we were our own worst enemy. After being on the attack we ended up passing the ball back to Green and then they won possession, again putting us under pressure. The best form of defence is attack, Leeds! The fans were fantastic from start to finish with great singing and a Roofe, Ayling and Berardi, Pontus Jansson's barmy army rendition going on for at least 10 minutes, which was quite a tongue-twister to begin with. (I'm hoping I got that right as I saw someone write Luke Ayling and Berardi, et cetera.) Green made two fantastic saves to keep Fulham out and there were a few nervous fans around me, although I did try to stay calm most of the time! We did have a chance to put the game to bed with a breakaway when the

Fulham A 7.3.17

Fulham A 7.3.17

ball should have been buried in the open goal, only for the ball to be too close to the post and rebounded off it. I honestly thought there was no way that the ball wasn't going to end up in the back of the net, unfortunately I was wrong. Just as we got to 90 minutes with Leeds battling as a team, Phillips was sent off when he tackled a Fulham player who reacted badly. I'm sure that's what got him sent off and will have to see a replay, but the lad was so upset when he went off. I was so disappointed for him. With five minutes of injury time shown it was obvious that Leeds were going to defend with being down to 10 men, but I wasn't sure how good we would be by doing that. Although we did break for a couple of attacks the ball kept running well for Fulham, and with time up and seconds left on the clock, Fulham shattered us with an equaliser. As soon as the ball left their player's boot at the edge of the penalty area you could see it was going in and Green had no chance. It was a killer blow, although at least it wasn't a winner, thank goodness. Yes, we had been riding our luck for a lot of the game, but to get so close to three points and end up with one was hard and a real shame.

Whilst we didn't get the three points, the team battled really well. Bridcutt, although giving the ball away, had defended well to prevent them scoring in the second half. Barrow needs to toughen up a bit, though, as he kept getting bundled off the ball by Fulham. All in all, we got a point out of the game which was always going to be difficult, despite the gut-wrenching timing of their equaliser. Fulham would have found it hard to get nothing out of the game, though, with all

Fulham A 7.3.17

Fulham A 7.3.17

the possession and chances they had. Still, I'm very proud of the Leeds United team and the fans today, which felt a bit like old-school Leeds. I loved the atmosphere, the singing and chanting, even telling Fulham to stick their clappers (sideways). Long-standing Leeds fans will know the words to that one!

As we headed back after the game I couldn't believe the sight of our disabled fans struggling on the long walk back to their coaches, with no assistance from the police. Some were parked so far away from the ground that I was disgusted to see that they hadn't been provided with some transport. Having seen some police forces look after these fans well in the past, I really feel that this is something that should be done automatically at all grounds and should be standard.

It was a late night made worse by motorway closures on both the M1 and A1, and then I was due to get up early for work in the morning. As it was I got home at 4.35 a.m., but as soon as my head hit the pillow, 15 minutes later I found myself wide awake. I got up and had a quick shower then went back to bed for one and a half hours before my alarm went off. Luckily, I managed better at work than I dared hope, although I was kept going with Pro Plus and black coffee! The things we do for Leeds!

Saturday sees us back at Elland Road for the visit of QPR and another big crowd getting behind Leeds. Just keep going Leeds, enjoy yourselves and play to our strengths, let the other teams worry about us! Another three points will do please – see you there – LUFC – Marching on Together!

QPR – 11 MARCH 2017

I was aiming to be at Elland Road earlier than usual, but by the time I'd picked my granddaughter Laura up it was 1.45 p.m. by the time we reached the Peacock. Another 30,000+ crowd was expected at Leeds today and the Peacock was packed. I had arranged to meet someone who was buying my book *Follow Me and Leeds United*. After trying to walk around the garden, I realised it was like looking for a needle in a haystack. Luckily, we managed to meet up, and a big thank you to Nick for the support.

It was a fine day and not too cold as we went into the ground around 15 minutes before kick-off. The team today was Green, Ayling, Berardi, Bartley, Jansson, Bridcutt, Vieira, Roofe, Wood, Pedraza and Hernandez. Subs were Sacko for Roofe, Doukara for Pedraza and O'Kane for Vieira. Attendance was 30,870, which in my eyes was 30,000 Leeds fans and approximately 870 QPR fans (maybe not even that many!). Today was also the 600th appearance for Green, and a big well done to him. He has been vital in our defence as of late, making some fantastic saves to keep out the opposition.

We had a couple of attacks which didn't come to anything before QPR started making the most of attacking us. Although they came close, luckily for us most of the shots went wide or over the crossbar, although with one cross they got in, I was sure Matt Smith was going to head it into our goal. He would have done but our defence more than matched him to clear the ball. There weren't any clear chances for us and although we came out strong from the back, we couldn't match that at the other end. QPR started time-wasting in the first half and were obviously here for a draw or a breakaway to win. What I wasn't happy to see was Pedraza going down like a sack of potatoes when I thought there was no need. He was very lucky not to get booked a couple of minutes later when it looked like he made a revenge tackle. I don't like diving and cheats and I may be doing him a disservice by thinking that's what he had done, but I stand by that, as it's something we don't need in our game. Especially when I've seen how other members of the team play out of their skins when battling for everything! As half-time approached I was just happy that QPR hadn't scored either.

The second half carried on in the same vein as the first. QPR weren't going to give up and make it easy for us. Unfortunately for us, we couldn't break them down, even though we did manage to have a lot of possession. As the lad next to me shouted when we won a corner, why have we got five players still back in our half? As I've said before, when Bridcutt plays we tend to play deep and to be honest it showed. We did attack, but their goalie really had very little to do (I think Green saw more action). We started putting more into the game from 60 minutes and the last 10 minutes saw us try to go for a win. When a great ball was put into the middle there were shouts for a penalty, as Wood claimed he was being held. We also should have had a corner with Doukara and their defender tackling on the line. The ref disagreed, though, and although I couldn't see the outcome I was told it was definitely a corner. When Sacko got into a great position to have a shot on goal in the final minutes he kept going across the edge of the area instead of having a go. In the end, he lost the ball when he could have at least tried to score. Luckily for us, though, QPR, despite getting into many scoring chances, were very poor with their final ball and did not have their shooting boots on. With QPR trying to slow the game down and get a point, they attacked our goal at the South Stand. I'm not sure what happened but there was a bit of squaring up which resulted in the game being stopped and O'Kane throwing one of their players to the floor twice! That was wrong timing and we shouldn't have risen to it, as we could have gone straight to the other end and scored. As it was, by the time the ref restarted the game (also after O'Kane and their player were booked due to the fourth official), the momentum was lost. He didn't play any extra time for the spat either.

I still think that no game is going to be easy and no other team is going to present us with three points every week. It was a frustrating game in the sense that I knew it wasn't going to get us a win. Yes, one point is better than none, which I will take as a positive as well as a clean sheet, even though in reality it feels like two points dropped. Well, my granddaughter Laura did say it would be a draw! Still, we just have to keep going and getting what points we can.

As we got back to near where I parked the car I saw a group of people around another car. As we reached it, I realised that the window had been smashed as there was glass everywhere, so I stopped to talk to them. I was told it was my fault by someone who knew me! The attack on the car was witnessed by a couple of women, one who had been asleep in her car across the road. She heard another woman screaming then realised what was going on. This happened half an hour before the end of the game. Whoever it was stole the radio console, so they knew what they were after, and got away through the woods. I know the police put out an alert the other week that fans had to be vigilant, so this has been going on for a good few weeks. There were more than enough police outside the ground at the end of the game, although with it being QPR I couldn't understand why. Surely there should be patrols going around so the thieves can be caught? I felt really sorry for the fans, especially when they have to drive back to Devon. Luckily they weren't going straight away, as they were going to some friends to get everything cleaned up first, but this will have soured their trip to Elland Road.

Next week sees our second home game in a week with the visit of Brighton. Thank you, BBC Radio Leeds, as I'd forgotten it was a 5.30 p.m. kick-off! As we have a few games where we play the teams around us I just want as many points as possible. The fact we have only nine games left to play this season is unbelievable. Where is the time going? With the international break after the Brighton game I wonder whether the impact this time will be good or bad for us. We normally seem to be on a good run and then can't pick ourselves up after the break, so this time, as things have been hit and miss (even though we are unbeaten in six games), I will accept us getting to the play-offs. See you next week – LUFC – Marching on Together!

BRIGHTON – 18 MARCH 2017

As it turned out I was very grateful that we had a late kick-off today, as I felt totally exhausted for some reason. At least it gave me chance to come round before I set off for Elland Road with my daughter Dani and granddaughter Hannah. Once in the Peacock, we met Per Steinar and his wife from Scandinavia. We have met Per many times before but it was the first time we had met his wife. She knows all about my friend Sue and me through my books that Per had bought, and it was nice to say hello. With the kick-off being later it was hard to work out what time we needed to go into the ground, but we ended up going in a lot earlier than usual. It was also good to bump into Paul Corrigan from Ireland, who helped me out with a ticket for our pre-season friendly in Dublin. With Brighton being in the top two of the table it was going to be another tough game today.

The team today was Green, Taylor, Cooper, Bartley, Berardi, Vieira, Bridcutt, Pedraza, Hernandez, Sacko and Wood. Subs were Doukara for Pedraza, Dallas for Sacko and O'Kane for Hernandez. It was a surprise to see Jansson on the bench but we thought he may be carrying an injury. Attendance was 29,767 with approximately 1,500 Brighton fans.

There was a great atmosphere around the ground today as we looked forward to a good game. The first thing Brighton did was turn us around, so we were attacking the Kop in the first half. That was a disappointment, but with vociferous Leeds fans behind both goals now it doesn't feel quite as bad as it used to do. For the first 20 minutes, though, we seemed to be doing a lot of passing along the back four as we played very deep. I know we like to pass the ball out from the back, but at times it was a little too close for comfort with Brighton closing us down quickly. I said to the lad next to me that we were only kidding! I did have a rant, though, after another close call and shouted 'what tactics are they being told to do?' As it was, we didn't have to wait long after that for us to start attacking, as we won our first corner of the game. We are a completely different team when we go forward rather than playing so deep. We had Green to thank again for pulling off a fantastic save, but what I didn't realise at the time was that it was from one of our players when Cooper was trying to clear the ball. There was some good banter between the Kop and the Brighton goalie Stockdale, who is known to be a Leeds fan. When we were chanting 'you're Leeds and you know you are' this had him turning round to us and smiling and eventually giving us a clap. I thought that was really good and nice to see. I think he is a good goalie too, although I didn't want him to keep us out today, but with no score at half-time that was fine.

The second half started with a lot faster pace than the first. We were attacking more but Brighton were always looking dangerous and had a couple of shots that Green was able to save with ease. We were having to battle hard to keep Brighton out, but with one of our next attacks we took the lead. Charlie Taylor crossed from the left and when Wood met the ball, almost in slow motion his looping header went over their goalie and into the net to send the Leeds fans wild once more! There was real hope that we would win this game, even though Brighton came close to

scoring shortly afterwards and Green made another fantastic save to deny them an equaliser. We were guilty of not releasing the ball to another of our players when on the attack, which resulted in losing the ball a few times. Once it gave Brighton the chance to break away but we defended brilliantly. We were able to put the game to bed when five minutes from the end of normal time we won a penalty. It was a definite penalty and Wood stepped up to power the ball into the net from the spot to claim his second goal of the game. There were eruptions all around Elland Road then with the celebrating Leeds fans and it was great to see and be a part of. In fact, Elland Road was bouncing! I was surprised to only see three minutes of extra time added on which passed very quickly. I would say the ref we had today was one of the better ones, letting the game flow even though he let some things go.

That was a good three points to get and keep us up there in the top six. I heard the Leeds fans shouting to Jansson, who had come onto the pitch with the others to cool down. Although he ran up and down the pitch he did not interact with the Leeds fans at all, which was very disappointing and not like him at all. I only hope nothing has gone on off the pitch but regardless, his reaction to the fans was not good.

Next week sees no game with the international break once again, before the trip to Reading the following week. This game sees another 5.30 p.m. kick-off but it will be nice to go and have a good day out with the rest of the Leeds fans. Keep going Leeds and play to our strengths, let other clubs worry about us! See you there LUFC – Marching on Together!

CHAPTER 10 – APRIL 2017

READING – 1 APRIL 2017

Not a great start as I was setting off to Reading, when I saw my car tyre was as flat as a... Just what I didn't need! Luckily, I had allowed myself plenty of time to get to Leeds for the coach as I tried to get a lift. I didn't want to drive the car, as although I knew it had a slow puncture that I was aiming to get sorted next week, the fact it had gone from full the previous night to zilch meant I didn't want to risk it.

After hurrying my other half up, who was having a shower first before taking me, he chastised me for my priorities. Well of course, I was catching a coach to Reading that was leaving Leeds in an hour! As we reached the M621 there were blue lights flashing on the opposite carriageway. Despite some traffic still passing by in the third lane that was gradually being stopped, the sight of a car with no roof on facing the other way meant things didn't look good. With the traffic straight away queuing up behind, it meant a detour home for my other half.

We had a decent journey down to Windsor, where we were visiting the Queen for our stop today. It's always a lovely place to visit and somewhere we have come for the last few years. That just reminded me of a conversation I had with my granddaughter Laura this week. She asked me if I was going to football this week, and I replied I'm going to London at the weekend. With that she said, Oma be careful on the bridge, four people were killed on it last week. I said I would, but the fact a six-year-old knew so much about the recent terrorist incident at Parliament saddens me greatly. Such a horrible thing to happen to the people involved too.

We had parked in the coach park, and although the castle looked a long walk away we were there in no time, coming up the steps next to the pub. We thought it was great to see a welcome for us Leeds fans with blue, yellow and white balloons everywhere. The landlord, a QPR fan, said it was because he knew we were coming! It was nice to get a friendly greeting. As I went to get a glass of water a couple of men started talking to me, saying the water had come straight out of the Thames, was full of vodka and there had been fishes swimming around in it recently! I still maintain that by wearing my Leeds things it always makes me approachable, as the amount of people who strike up a conversation is great. It happened again when I went for a further glass of water and I had a conversation with a Crystal Palace fan who introduced himself as Paul, and another chap. I said I hoped to have my flag up in the ground and Paul had said there shouldn't be any issues with that, so I told them to look out for it on TV. A big thank you to Ella for buying my book *Follow Me and Leeds United*, and it's nice to see the younger generation of Leeds fans taking an interest in following Leeds in the seventies. I was a female in a man's world at that time but I wouldn't change it for anything in the world (apart from all the trouble) as I had the privilege of seeing the best team ever play. Billy Bremner always was and always will be my hero!

As we pulled off the M25 and queued on the short journey to the ground, which took ages, all of a sudden all the fans behind us on the coach were shouting he didn't touch you. There had been a small bump and the second car had a Leeds fan driving. Not a good start to the game for him. As we pulled up at the ground we found out that Burton had scored in the 97th minute to win against Huddersfield. Our coach dropped us off more or less outside the turnstiles and we got in the ground very quickly. With approximately 20 mins until kick-off, I put my flag up behind the goal before heading up to my seat. We also heard Jansson hadn't got off the team coach either when he'd been with the squad earlier. I'd seen a tweet earlier saying he'd tweeted a transfer then deleted it but assumed it was an April fool, then heard it was a hamstring issue. Whatever is going on in the background, I feel it is to the detriment of the team. Also, I feel there is a lot of spin going on again, sadly.

The team today was Green, Berardi, Taylor, Bartley, Cooper, Vieira, Bridcutt, Hernandez, Sacko, Pedraza and Wood. Subs were Doukara for Sacko, Phillips for Pedraza and Roofe for Vieira. Attendance was 23,055 with 3,546 Leeds fans. I'd seen a Reading tweet earlier saying today's game was a sell-out, to which I'd responded, 'You're only here to watch the Leeds.' Therefore it was a big surprise to see so many fans disguised as seats in the Reading end! There had also been a lot of brinksmanship going on before the game with Stam the Reading manager. When the game kicked off the Leeds fans started singing something which I thought at first was something about a family club. I realised how bad my hearing had got with the recognition of what they were actually singing, oops.

I had high hopes that despite the international break we would turn up for this game. It took only 20 minutes to realise that this was not the case. Although both teams didn't start off well, we seemed to be standing off Reading, preferring to watch rather than get stuck in. Because of this it gave Reading the chance to start putting us under pressure, but at that time it seemed they'd left their shooting boots at home. But that didn't last long, as they took a quick throw which concluded with a goal despite Green's efforts to keep the goal out. Reading had the luck of the ball running for them and two or three of our players being unable to get rid of the ball. Despite this we had a couple of chances, and we really should have buried them. You cannot afford to miss these, as opportunities were few and far between. We got a corner and proceeded to waste it by taking a short one. When you can't get into the box that's a mistake, I feel. Just before the whistle blew for half-time Reading broke away and, luckily for us, the ball hit the post with Green beaten and bounced away. The first half had been absolutely dire, though.

The start of the second half saw a more positive start and Wood started to put Reading under pressure. This also saw the ref get worse. He had not let the game flow in the first half but was guilty of letting play carry on when fouls were committed against us. He was terrible and already had a reputation of never doing well against us prior to the game. Every little push was given against us, then Reading resorted to cheating to slow the game down and waste time when their player went down like a sack of spuds with a non-injury! Time-wasting but damn right cheating, which I hate! The

Leeds fans were getting very angry, which was understandable, but why all of a sudden we have some throwing bottles onto the pitch is not. Come on, we are better than that, we don't need to have any repercussions coming our way through doing it. This happened at least four times, unfortunately. The last two when I was standing near the front, having gone down for my flag. The worried look on the female steward's face meant I told her I was going to get my flag and not run on the pitch. To be fair she was decent and let me get it. I did clap the players off the pitch despite my disappointment with the result. Having met Valencia White, Scandinavian Whites and Dublin Whites they probably had more reason to be disappointed, with the miles they had travelled to the game!

The journey home was a nightmare with diversions sending us all over the country, well, it felt like it! Fingers crossed we've gone through the last one at 23.30! With Brentford away and then Preston at Elland Road next Saturday, I feel this will be a big week points-wise. I never take anything for granted and want as many points as possible. Our tactics today were very poor in my opinion and the team choice wasn't good either. I feel if we'd have come out and put Reading under pressure from the start then they would have crumbled. It's a shame the weak shot from Doukara that was fumbled by their keeper and went under his body was on the wrong side of the post, too! Never mind, luckily for me I forget how bad things have been very easily. I also said I was going daft as well as deaf. As the board went up at half-time with the stoppage time, I glanced at the TV screen to the right of me and saw 18.16. I thought no way is it only 18 minutes into the game, as that means it will be a long game. As I looked again I realised it said 44 minutes to the right of the screen. As I exclaimed out loud that I'd looked at the time on the left instead of the minutes played on the right, it brought a laugh from everyone around me, although one said it was my age, lol! I found out later that some others were confused by it too so I wasn't the only one.

Tuesday will be the anniversary of my baby daughter's death, and amidst my sorrow my heart will go out to the families and friends of Christopher Loftus and Kevin Speight, who were tragically killed in Turkey. All will never be forgotten, RIP.

At least I managed to get home, and a big thank you to both my daughter Emily and future son-in-law Alex for picking me up when I got back to Leeds. Instead of mum's taxi it was taxi for mum! See you next week LUFC – Marching on Together!

BRENTFORD – 4 APRIL 2017

I was glad that I'd have plenty to occupy me today, as it marks the anniversary of my baby daughter's death. Amidst those sorrows, all Leeds fans will be remembering the families and friends of Christopher Loftus and Kevin Speight on the eve of their tragic deaths in Turkey. Always in our hearts, gone but never forgotten. MOT.

A big thank you once again for the help from fans who gave me the chance to get to the game, as always that is greatly appreciated. As it was, we made it to the ground in good time and didn't encounter any hold-ups, thank goodness.

Brentford A 4.4.17

It was nice to catch up with some friends in the Griffin pub by the away end. It was also nice to see both sets of fans mixing with no issues. It was funny to see that fans were getting served at the back window of the pub at the same time as a police forensics officer was working underneath it. Apparently the pub had been broken into during the previous night, and whilst sorry to hear that, as Leeds fans were getting served they were putting fingerprints on the area that was being checked for…you've guessed it, fingerprints! You couldn't make it up really, but as long as those queuing for booze don't get a knock on the door…Valencia White was there again and his mates were laughing that all he'd brought with him for his trip to the UK was his toothbrush. Then we had a laugh as he was wearing three T-shirts, two pairs of socks and undies and was mixing and matching! He asked if he smelt and then said, 'Forget that, lol!' He's here until the Newcastle game so maybe he'll have cadged a bath by then. But as he slept rough one night to raise money for charity, he will know how to survive and he's a good lad. I made my way into the pub and didn't realise there was a side door until I'd struggled through the crowd of fans. I went out that way as I wasn't going to make the same mistake. I'd had loads of fans speaking to me, some who told me they really enjoy reading my blogs so a big thank you to them. I then saw Collar and had a good chat with him before I headed into the ground just before kick-off.

Before the game we'd heard that Cooper was being charged due to him stamping on a Reading player's face last Saturday. Whilst I couldn't disagree with the charge in retrospect, the fact one of the Reading players got away with a forearm smash on Wood in the same game wasn't right, as he should have faced a charge too. Because Cooper pleaded guilty to the charge it meant he was banned from tonight's game. Whenever anyone asked what I thought the score would be, I told them I wasn't confident of getting a result here as we didn't have a good record against them.

The team was Green, Berardi, Ayling, Jansson, Bartley, Barrow, Hernandez, Dallas, Wood, Bridcutt and Phillips. Subs were Pedraza for Dallas, Roofe for Barrow and Doukara for Bridcutt. Attendance was 10,759 with approximately 1,700 Leeds fans.

We started off quite brightly and it was noticeable that Bridcutt was getting stuck in, unlike at Reading. Ayling had come back into the team after his suspension and I thought that he was getting roasted by their player every time they attacked, and was constantly caught out of position. Now, I like Ayling, but it seemed as though the suspension had had an effect on his performance. We struggled to get any momentum going forward, though. Suddenly, after 16 minutes, we were up against it once more. Although it wasn't a good view of the goal we were defending from the seats above the terracing, I saw Green make a great save, only for the rebound to go straight to a Brentford player who put the ball into the net. Before we knew it we were two goals down, despite the heroics of Green who was to end up my man of the match, making some crucial saves to keep the scoreline down. Any shots we had were tame in comparison, unfortunately. At half-time the fans I spoke to weren't very happy with the way things were going.

Despite coming out more up for it at the start of the second half, I don't think we'd have scored if we'd have stayed there for a month of Sundays. Although having just read that Jansson had a

header cleared off the line, which couldn't be seen from my seat, I would gladly have been proved wrong. The consensus amongst the Leeds fans I spoke to felt that something has happened behind the scenes, as we didn't look like a team playing for each other as we have done in the past. The game was littered with errors and players who had looked solid previously seemed jittery. I said we should forget any talk of going up, because as soon as we get near to anything we self-destruct. I realise there is still a chance at this stage, but I'm going to try reverse psychology in the fact that we should pretend we are just trying to get into a play-off position instead! Sorry, but on the whole this was another poor and rubbish performance, and I felt sorry for the lad from Greece and the couple from Norway stood next to me at the game. When I think how far they have travelled to see the terrible performance today and at Reading, I don't think I've anything to complain about despite the miles travelled to the game. Many Leeds fans left the game saying how rubbish it had been and asking for my opinion, where I agreed with the rubbish statement. After another tour around the country due to shut motorways, I finally got into bed at 3.00 a.m. with a few hours' sleep before work. Many other fans were still on the road at that time, though.

Our next couple of games really are crucial now, with Preston first on Saturday and the return of Simon Grayson and Glynn Snodin. As our ex-manager returns, I don't think I'm under any illusions as to what is heading our way, especially as they won 5–0 today and seem to be scoring for fun. Let's hope that we can be up for it again with another big crowd behind us. We really need to get back to winning ways otherwise we may as well forget about promotion this season altogether. Monk and the team have overachieved for certain and I'm grateful for the fact that I've begun to enjoy the football once again, rather than being resigned to losing all the time. Interestingly, in my opinion, since we've reverted to playing deeper with the return of Bridcutt into the side, our play as a team seems to have suffered. Our best form of defence is attack, so maybe it's time to revert to what helped us start on our winning run.

We'll have to be the twelfth man on Saturday, and I know we can do this as Leeds fans in full voice at both ends of the stadium are awesome. Simon and Glynn know all about our fans, though, with both supporting Leeds too, but I'm hoping we can scare the Preston team to death, so to speak. See you there LUFC – Marching on Together!

PRESTON – 8 APRIL 2017

I'd sent a tweet to LUFC this morning: 'Come on Leeds, a win today will keep our hopes alive #LUFC @LUFC Perfect weather for football at Elland Road, see you there!'

The weather was glorious as I went to pick up my granddaughter Hannah. The difference it makes to a footballing day is unbelievable in my opinion, as it made me feel upbeat and more positive than of late. We were looking forward to another 30,000+ crowd to roar the team on and it was perfect conditions for a home game. The Peacock was packed out with lots of fans outside enjoying the sunshine and there was a positive feel about the place.

Preston H 8.4.17

As we headed into the ground I saw a couple of policemen with a little boy who said he was lost. As they asked where he had last been with his dad, he said the shop. I said he was probably queuing and still in the shop. With that a man came across and said he knew the lad's dad and then a woman came over and said she had seen him queuing in the shop by the printing. I'm sure he got reunited very quickly but this was Leeds fans at their best, all out to help each other. We got into the ground before kick-off and once the team were out, both teams headed to the centre circle for a minute's applause. With the 17th anniversary since the tragic deaths of Christopher Loftus and Kevin Speight in Turkey last Wednesday, their photos were put up on the screen as the whole ground rose as one to pay tribute to them both. I had to stifle a sob as I found this so emotional (one of my friends said the same at half-time). RIP lads, and thoughts with your families and friends.

The team today was Green, Ayling, Bartley, Jansson, Berardi, Vieira, Phillips, Pedraza, Hernandez, Wood and Roofe. Subs were Dallas for Roofe, Doukara for Wood and Taylor for Hernandez. Attendance was 31,851 with approximately 1,800 Preston fans.

In my blog from last Tuesday at Brentford I had said: 'Interestingly, in my opinion, since we've reverted to playing deeper with the return of Bridcutt into the side, our play as a team seems to have suffered. Our best form of defence is attack, so maybe it's time to revert to what helped us start on our winning run.' Bridcutt wasn't playing today due to an injury to his Achilles (according to BBC Radio Leeds) and to be honest we didn't play as deep and had an attacking side to our

game. We set off at a fast pace but in the first 15 minutes Preston had the chance to put the game to bed, having a few chances including a one to one that Green pulled off another fantastic save to deprive them of a goal. Green has shown to me just how much he has grown into the position this year and looks so self-assured, even jumping high to catch the ball when under pressure from their attack. I am so glad that he has been in goal this year, giving us some stability in that position. One thing I will say is that for this stage of the season, the pitch is in a fantastic state and is very good to see. The amount of times in the past that it was threadbare in front of the goal and other places shows the difference.

The fans in the crowd were in good voice, getting behind the team, and this is what is needed to put the opposition under pressure rather than have a quiet stadium. We had been turned round again at the start with us attacking the Kop in the first half, which isn't as much a jinx as it used to be. We started putting our attacks together when we were winning the ball in defence and using our wings to move forwards. Ayling was a completely different person to Tuesday, as he was attacking down the wing. We were playing as a team once again and backing each other up and fighting for the ball, which was good to see. After another good move coming forward Roofe put the ball into the net, to put us into the lead within 20 minutes. Getting an early goal was always going to be vital, in my opinion. We kept attacking after this and played some great football, including some great passing. Just before half-time Chris Wood put the ball into the net to put us 2–0 up, or so we thought, until the ref went to speak to the linesman and disallowed it, for offside I think. That was very disappointing, especially as it was so close to half-time, and I really hoped that decision wouldn't backfire on us. I needn't have worried, because with another attack Hernandez seemed to fall as he hit the ball past the advancing goalkeeper. Even though the ball was travelling very slowly, it was good to see it have enough momentum to go into the net before the Preston players could scoop it out. What a great feeling to know we had scored two goals (three really) before half-time and it felt more comfortable than a one-goal lead.

At the start of the second half, Preston came out fighting and to start with the crowd wasn't as vociferous as they had been in the first half. It took approximately five minutes before we found our voices again, so luckily it wasn't for long. Not long after that we were very unlucky not to get another goal when Wood's attempt came back off the crossbar. We had a few more chances which came close before Grayson, now the manager for Preston, made a double substitution with Beckford coming on. Beckford had been welcomed by the Leeds fans chanting his name almost hero-like, but ensuring he was remembered for his goal at Old Trafford in the FA Cup 3rd round when we beat man u. 'You're Leeds and you know you are,' was also chanted when he had been warming up, and when he turned back to the Kop he gave us a quick clap! The substitutions put us under pressure for quite a spell, though, as the minutes were ticking by and we had Green to thank again for making a great save before the crossbar saved us from the rebound. Doukara had a good chance and should have done better. As Taylor was due to come on as sub, Hernandez was fouled near the corner by the cheese wedge. As I followed the direction of the ball I only heard everyone going mad as my daughter said, did he just stamp on him? I don't know where Hernandez was stamped on but the referee had no hesitation in sending the Preston player off. The same player had seemed very angry early on, so had his just desserts by getting sent off. Straight away before the free-kick was taken Taylor came on and went to left-back. Berardi was on the right wing with Ayling playing to the left of him and both marking the tall, blond-haired Preston player. Luckily for us the pressure was taking off us with the sending off and then to crown it all, when the ball was passed through for Doukara we got the rub of the green. He advanced with the ball and beat their goalie on the near post to give us a third goal on the day. That was it, game over in our favour and the three points that we really needed to get today to keep us in with a chance of the play-offs.

The players came around the pitch at the end of the game as Jansson engaged with the fans in the South Stand first. As he approached the East Stand he took his shirt off and then took hold of the Swedish flag as he gave his shirt away. After posing with the flag he gave it back, and then engaged with the fans in the Kop too. It was a welcome sight as he had also had a good game too, as well as the whole team. My granddaughter had said how good it was to know there were Leeds fans from other countries at the game. I told her we had a worldwide fan base as she tried to reel off the places where Leeds fans come from. At Billy's statue after the game there were some Leeds fans from Mexico, which she thought was fantastic. Just before we'd got there it was funny seeing the police escort for some Preston fans, where there was nearly as many police as fans!

The win today couldn't have come at a better time, with us playing Newcastle on Good Friday in our next game. It will be another hard game, that's for sure, but we have to go into the game playing to our strengths and not to be scared of them by standing off them. We need to approach the game in the same way as today and you never know, we may upset the apple cart! I may not be looking forward to climbing the mountain of steps to our seats on the seventh level, but with the rest of the Leeds fans travelling up there, another three points would make our day. You never know – see you there, LUFC – Marching on Together!

NEWCASTLE – 14 APRIL 2017

It's been a pretty stressful week. Being sat at a funeral wake on Tuesday to hear my granddaughter was on her way to hospital from the doctor's, to rule out meningitis, meant everything else went out of the window. Whilst I wouldn't wish acute tonsillitis on her, the relief to know it was that rather than meningitis was overwhelming, especially as it came so soon after the anniversary of my daughter's death. After going straight to the hospital to join them, I was happy when she was discharged.

After the win against Preston I was more optimistic for our trip to Newcastle today. As long as we don't give them the respect we did at Elland Road and standoff them, we could upset the apple cart tonight. As I set off for Elland Road, the butterflies and knots started in my stomach and by the time I reached Shibden Park I felt quite emotional. I realised then how much the game and result meant to me. After queuing for ages at Wyke garage due to a crash at the traffic lights, it gave me time to reflect and made me glad that I had allowed myself plenty of time to get to Leeds. As the ambulance was already there I realised that it hadn't happened long before I got there, but hopefully the people involved in the crash were okay, although seeing the stretcher being unloaded meant there were some injuries.

As I parked up at Elland Road I realised that there were a lot of families around, but it wasn't until I headed to Billy's bar that I realised it was for the ground tours as John McClelland led them out of there.

Our stop today was at Green Hammerton before making our own way to the game. Hooray, as that meant no police escort from Washington services. Whilst I've no objection to the escorts, being kept there until 7 p.m. before getting escorted in was a joke last time we were there. We arrived at the ground at kick-off and I proceeded to run up the first three flights of stairs then staggered up the rest. I realised I wasn't fit enough to run up 14 flights of stairs, and then had another load of steps to get to my seat! To be honest, I would hate to have a seat that high up permanently, as it is too far away from the pitch, not a good view of a football game or being part of it for me.

We had only been travelling for 40 minutes when I started feeling really hot, sweaty and feeling sick. I had to take off my beret which is normally glued to my head and my waistcoat to try and cool down. I was so glad we didn't have long to wait until our stop. Hopefully it was more travel sickness than anything else but I didn't feel well at all, and even felt like lying down in the aisle rather than being in my seat! I was so glad when we pulled up at the club and got straight to the front ready to get off into the fresh air. I did this and then had to hang on to the side of the coach as everything started to go black around me. As I was nearly passing out I was very grateful for Richard helping me across the road and a big thank you to him. I'd sent a message to my friend Sue to have a pint of water ready for me and sat outside to drink it. Eventually, after having a further couple of pints of water and some pie and peas, normality returned. We decided later on that I'd been dehydrated and my induction trip to the gym yesterday, along with another hour-long class I did, was probably too much.

I decided the best way to try and forget how I'd been feeling was to start taking photos and talking about Leeds! We had the Welsh Whites stopping at the club too so had a great chat with some of them. A big thank you to Brian Bevan, the Number 1 referee in Wales, for buying my book *Follow Me and Leeds United*! I'll look forward to getting his feedback, but we all had a laugh discussing memories, including his own refereeing exploits! It was a really nice few hours spent before we departed for the ground. As the A1 was really bad traffic wise, we went up the A19 and couldn't believe how easy the journey was in comparison.

We pulled up on the road leading to the ground, and as quite a few of the fans headed for the pub opposite where we'd parked we headed into the ground. I remember our exploits in the

Magpie pub opposite the ground all those years ago. I'd had a conversation with Richard earlier (who'd helped me when I was ill) saying that we wouldn't be kicked out of there today! A group of us had gone in there in the seventies, and although the Newcastle fans had chanted how much they hated us it wasn't until we left to go to the game that things kicked off. We lasses got out okay but Richard and another lad got literally kicked out of it! Mick Bates had got me a couple of complimentary tickets for that game but we were so scared, we daren't go near the players' entrance after that!

The team today was Green, Ayling, Berardi, Bartley, Jansson, Hernandez, Bridcutt, Phillips, Pedraza, Wood and Roofe. Subs were Sacko for Pedraza, Doukara for Bridcutt and Taylor for Berardi. Attendance was 52,301 with approximately 3,000 Leeds fans. I took it steady climbing all the stairs to level 7, but some fans struggled with it. The good thing is, at least there is a lift for our disabled and other fans who would not be able to climb the stairs. To be honest, if I hadn't have come round from earlier I'd have been in the lift too! I was pleasantly surprised to see we were on the balcony and on row C, right behind the goal. It was a lot better view than I'd hoped for and not as high as before. Because I'd felt ill before I sat down for most of the game. A big thank you also for the Leeds badge I was given.

As expected with the tough game ahead, Leeds were put under plenty of pressure at the start of the game. We nearly took the lead with our first attack of the game as we hit the crossbar and had the ball cleared off the line. Although we didn't do much attacking, I thought we were defending well. In fact, it became one of those games where our backs were against the wall but we were playing as a team and defending well despite all the attacking Newcastle were doing. Green again shows how important he is to the team, making some fantastic saves, and I know we are in safe hands with him. Although Newcastle nearly scored when the ball hit the post after a mistake from Hernandez, it was good to know we had kept the score level at half-time. For once in my life I felt quite bolshie, and felt that as long as we kept going and didn't give up we could get something out of the game. The Leeds fans had been in good voice during the first half and we had a new Vieira song, although I couldn't understand the second line. It wasn't until I lip-read some fans as I was going onto the concourse at half-time, that I realised what the whole song was: Ooooohhh Ronaldo Vieira, Oooooohhh he's only a teenager, Oooooohhhh he never gives the ball away, 1234 – rinse and repeat as someone else said!

The second half was more of the same, with constant Newcastle pressure and some great defending from Leeds. Jansson showed more than once how important he was in our defence, along with Green. Although it was a mistake from Sacko when his pass wasn't strong enough that saw Newcastle take the lead. Green made a fantastic save but unfortunately for us it had gone over the line, although it wasn't far into the goal it was enough for it to be given. I stood up then for the rest of the game, as old habits die hard. This was the wakeup call for the Newcastle fans to start chanting and singing. To be honest, they had been very poor and not very vocal, although for the

next 10 minutes the noise was deafening from them. Sing when you're winning comes to mind! It probably took that long for the Leeds fans to get going again but they got behind the team. With all the diving from some of the Newcastle players I'd thought we'd be lucky not to concede a penalty, so the fact the goal came from open play was better. You could tell they'd been in the premiership recently. Overpriced players throwing themselves about and trying to cheat their way through games is not what I like to see. I'd not given up, though, and felt we could still get something out of the game as we deserved it. It reminded me of the Don Revie days and Billy and the lads defending for their lives in some of the European games. It was a case of not losing this game either and if it meant by defending this way, then so be it. When Bridcutt went off we moved higher up the pitch, and with Newcastle wasting time we started coming forwards and attacking. The ball was cleared from Newcastle before coming back to Hernandez who put the ball out wide to Roofe, whose cross was met by the one and only Chris Wood and the ball was in the net. Cue delirious scenes of joy on the terraces above the goal with the Leeds fans going mental, and me saying I knew we could do it! What a fantastic ending for us and fully deserved as far as I was concerned. The team deserved their plaudits at the end of the game. Wood was the last man off the pitch after being interviewed by Sky TV.

It was great singing the Vieira song going out of the ground. As we got to the bottom of the stairs underneath the stand I realised we had a welcoming committee at the other side of the stand. Although it was cordoned off between the two sets of fans with police and stewards, it always looked like things were going to kick off. At one point, I'm sure the Newcastle fans broke through the cordon, but I knew the Leeds fans would stand between us and they wouldn't get near me. There was quite a crush at this point and it seemed to take ages to get out of the ground. As we were going back to the coaches I met a couple from Melton Mowbray who were on our coach. They couldn't find it but I said we were quite far up the road. They followed me but we kept going for what seemed ages and I hoped it hadn't been moved at that point! Luckily we got there eventually, but it was a relief to know we'd got back to it okay. I'd heard a lad shouting SLI do you know where the coach is, as he ran back past us. I feel there were a few who couldn't find their coach for a while.

It wasn't until we set off and got near the pub that we saw the police surrounding a lad laid out in the middle of the road. He wasn't moving, and as Leeds fans were around him we assumed he was one of our fans. There were fans lined up outside the pub which the Leeds fans had gone in earlier, which we thought were Geordies. I hope the lad is okay, but as an ambulance passed us not long after, Sue and I assumed it was the lad being taken to hospital. Fingers crossed as he looked in a bad way.

Today was a welcome point as we head into our game with Wolves on Monday. I will be heading to Selby market in the morning with my family before we head to Elland Road for the game. We will all be wearing our Leeds things, as my elder daughter Michelle and three granddaughters join me and my daughter Danielle at the game. My youngest granddaughter Alexis, aged three, keeps pointing to the Leeds badge on my shirt every time she sees it and shouts Leeds, Leeds! Well we couldn't disappoint her, so I'm hoping to see Lucas the Kop Cat for a photo with them all!

As we run out of games at the end of the season, let's just enjoy ourselves and let other teams worry about us as we play to our strengths. At the end of next week with the Burton away game, we will have a better idea of where we are. Fingers crossed things go our way, see you on Monday – LUFC – Marching on Together!

WOLVES – 17 APRIL 2017

When I arrived back from the Newcastle game I found I was wide awake for most of the night so I only had a couple of hours sleep, probably due to buzzing about our ending to the game. Last night I found I couldn't sleep either due to an active mind, but also knowing I had to be up early as we were heading to Selby market first.

Although I was intending to get to the Peacock before the game, due to not getting to the ground until 2.35 p.m. I decided to just go straight into the ground. I headed in with my granddaughter Hannah, as my daughters Michelle and Dani followed with my other two granddaughters, Laura and Alexis. We weren't all in the same stand today but the little ones were looking forward to the game.

Wolves H 17.4.17

Wolves H 17.4.17

As we got into the stand we headed to behind the goal, where I was meeting Shaun Stone and his girlfriend who were here from London to celebrate his birthday. The last time Shaun was here he was able to see everything, but unfortunately now wasn't able to due to deterioration of his vision. Already this morning they had been on a tour of the ground and had met some of the players, so I'm glad things had gone well. After this I was waiting at the front of the stand to see little Olly from the West Midlands coming out with the team. He was one of the mascots, in a proud moment for both him and his dad. Olly has had many hurdles to overcome over the years and is now able to play football too, something that was beyond him for a long time. A great day for all concerned regardless of the final score.

The team today was Green, Jansson, Bartley, Berardi, Ayling, Bridcutt, Roofe, Pedraza, Wood, Phillips and Hernandez. Subs were Sacko for Bridcutt, Taylor for Berardi and Doukara for Pedraza. Attendance was 32,351 with approximately 1,000 Wolves fans.

Conditions were pretty good as the sun came out, but Wolves won the toss and turned us around to attack the Kop in the first half. Although it hasn't impacted on us too much in the recent games when this has happened, for once it didn't take long to realise that this was going to be a long afternoon. Wolves had come to attack us and put us under pressure and we couldn't cope with things at all. I got a sinking feeling very quickly and just expected Wolves to score first, although I hoped if that happened we would be able to come from behind and still win the game. It was noticeable that we were playing deep again and that things weren't working out in our midfield. We had Green to thank once again for another brilliant save before we woke up after the half hour mark and started to attack ourselves. We had shouts for a penalty turned down when Bartley was fouled in the area and it looked as if we were up for a fight, only for things to take a turn for the worse. From a Leeds attack with Jansson still up-field, Wolves countered with their own attack and put the ball into the net to put them into the lead just before half-time. This felt very predictable, though, and my worst fears were realised, sadly.

We started the second half on the attack and looked lively for a while. We had another claim for a penalty turned down for handball (memories of Wolves playing pat-a-ball in the penalty area at Molineux in 1972 came flooding back!) before coming close with a couple of chances. I just felt there was no way we were going to score as my fatigue set in and I was glad when the game came to an end. It was a disappointing game, and overall I think we played very poorly. More often than not our passing was poor and didn't reach our players. We did start attacking more once Bridcutt then Berardi were subbed, but despite the number of corners we had we couldn't beat the first man most times. A great corner in would have put their goalie and defence under pressure, but we failed to deliver.

As we headed to Billy's statue for some photos, as we were too late to get them when we arrived, I started talking to a lad from Barlow who reads my blogs. We both have had trauma in our lives and it is good when people open up and talk about things, as I think that is a great healer. I am always approachable and have broad shoulders for chats like the one we had. Our result today

Wolves H 17.4.17

has meant that we have come out of the play-off positions on goal difference. Despite me thinking we only had one game left for some reason, there are still twists and turns to come with all the teams in contention. Whether or not we get into the play-offs I cannot say, as only time will tell. Many fans have faith we can do this, whereas I will take each game as it comes and try not to jinx anything by saying we can definitely do it!

Burton away beckons on Saturday, and it will be my first trip there as I was on holiday the last time we played a friendly there. Another new ground to add to the many I have visited over the years. Our last home game the week after against Norwich, then Wigan away as our last game means we will shortly know our fate. Whatever happens, with the season ticket renewals out we will get ours sorted as soon as we can, as the money has been saved up ready to go. As Leeds United fans, we know there are always ups and downs where we are concerned, but I would much prefer to go up automatically than through the lottery of the play-offs. Unfortunately, as we have no choice in the matter, our outcome will be provided for us. See you at Burton – LUFC – Marching on Together!

BURTON – 22 APRIL 2017

Today I was picking up Jo in Halifax, so I had some company on my way to Leeds. After travelling with Jo to Cambridge earlier in the season, we had a good sing-song both on the way there and back, so I put a *Heartbeat* CD on for us to enjoy. As we were on the coach ready to leave Elland Road I was talking to my friend Sue, when in mid-sentence I shouted, 'What the hell are you doing there!' Well, of course, a lone magpie had decided to land on the Peacock fence and I couldn't believe it. Of course the superstitions arose, but I said, 'No, we are not letting that happen today!'

Our stop today was in Chesterfield and it didn't take us long to get there. It was very busy for a while but we managed to find some seats. I'd gone back to the bar to queue, and as I was stood there this lad to the left of me ran out of the pub saying, I'm not stopping it's going to kick-off! I realised there were a group of them, including a couple of lasses, so I asked who they were. They were Derby fans on their way to Sheffield Wednesday. I assured them there would be no kicking off from any of us, and also said no doubt there would be Leeds fans in the other pubs anyway. Tony bought my co-authored book *The Good, The Bad and The Ugly of Leeds United* for his son and a big thank you for the support. We arrived at the ground in good time and passed the Beech pub, which I think has Leeds fans running it. After a chat to big Mick Hewitt I went into the ground and kept talking to people so only got into the stand five minutes before kick-off.

There were changes to the team today: Green, Ayling, Bartley, Jansson, Taylor, Phillips, Vieira, Wood, Doukara, Roofe and Hernandez. Subs were Sacko for Doukara and Pedraza for Phillips. Attendance was 6,073 with approximately 1,600 Leeds fans. There was also a beam back of the game at Elland Road.

Burton A 22.4.17

Burton A 22.4.17

It was a nice sunny day as the game kicked off, although there was a lot of apprehension in the air from the Leeds fans. Some were really positive, whereas I was going to take things as they came. We started off quite well and it wasn't long before we had the ball in the net. As I was just going to zoom in on the players celebrating I realised the fans' arms in front of me had gone down, as the goal had been disallowed. As it was too far away to see why, I will look forward to seeing highlights later. Instead of this giving us the impetus, though, and getting us fired up, it was Burton who seemed to be getting into the game more. We had a lot of passes going astray as the anxiety amongst the players took hold. The score remained goalless at half-time, but as many fans had heard that Fulham were winning at Huddersfield the mood was quite sombre. The Leeds fans had tried to get things going many a time but you could sense that there was a lot of apprehension about. As I spoke to Greeny at half-time, he said things had a déjà vu about them as we had been in this position before. I said I couldn't see us doing it sadly, as I'd had a gut feeling things wouldn't work for us.

In the second half Leeds were attacking the goal to our right where the Leeds fans on the terraces were. We were close to the pitch and had a good view at this end. One cross from Charlie Taylor at the far side of the pitch was pinpointed right to the top of Chris Wood's head, only for a defender to get in front of him. We did have a couple of chances and I said, as things could go either way at the time, the first goal would tell which way it was going. On 75 minutes we heard the Burton fans for the first time since the start of the game, and for some reason it had an effect as the ball ended up in our net. I'd also just said their players had long legs whilst our players had short legs, but as they persevered they got around our players to score. If that wasn't all, it didn't take long before they got a second. The consensus from many angry fans was that we had bottled it and thrown it away. I said maybe we could make a comeback, then we scored a goal from Bartley to pull one back. Although we came close to scoring another a bit later, we were destined to our second defeat in a week.

As we were walking back to the coaches a lad said he'd just bought my second book *Once a Leeds fan, always a Leeds fan* on his Kindle, so unfortunately I couldn't autograph that for him! I'd arranged to see Allen, one of the Welsh lads, at the game as he wanted my book *Follow Me and Leeds United*. I thought I'd seen him in the opposite side of the ground to me but thought I'd have to post it out to him. All of a sudden, he appeared at the side of me, so a big thank you to Allen too. As with any of the books, I look forward to receiving feedback about them in due course.

Whilst I realise we hadn't played well in many games this season, for some reason we got points that kept us up in the top six for a long while. Yes, it is gutting that we have got so near but yet so far, but I would hate to see us play like this in a play-off or at Wembley, as well as the money it would cost us. If we were by some miracle to still get there I would take it, but as I say, gut feelings tell me otherwise. It is such a shame, but if this is to be the case then we need to go all out next season and get automatic promotion, never mind depending on play-offs! Whether this happens at all depends so much on what happens next at Leeds over the next few weeks. With so many players on loans or not signed contracts, including Monk, we look to be teetering on a knife edge once again. For once I want us to have stability and build on what we have got. Starting again by getting rid of most of the team is not an option at all! We as fans have shown how good our support is and how we will back the team and the club, and now we shall see what happens with this 50:50 ownership. Whether MC goes in June as suggested, only time will tell. Also, with the full house signs up for the Norwich home game next week, we really have nothing to play for now, but as they say, until the fat lady stops singing there is always a chance! See you there LUFC – Marching on Together.

NORWICH – 29 APRIL 2017

I'd put my *Yorkshire Evening Post* Leeds shirt on today as a tribute to the Last Champions – Leeds United in 1992! Being pregnant in those final days I will always have a constant reminder of the year, as my daughter Danielle is pictured with her dad and the Cup when she was five weeks old. Bring them up as Leeds right from the start, and she is still Leeds to this day!

As we headed to Elland Road for our last home game of the season, the sun was trying to come out and warm things up for us but it felt a good day for football. There were five of us today with my other half, two daughters Michelle and Danielle and granddaughter Laura. We'd made arrangements to get there early for once and arrived at Elland Road by 1.30 p.m. With a sell-out

Leeds crowd it was going to be busy. The Peacock was heaving but I decided to queue up and get a drink and had a chat with a few people I knew. Also, a girl spoke to me who had received my first book *Follow Me and Leeds United* for Christmas, so it was nice to get some feedback from her. There was a buzz about the place which was made even better by having a rendition of 'Marching on Together' by the band in the garden just before I left. It never fails to move me when everyone sings along to it. Just as I was leaving I bumped into some of the Norwegians over for the game, who were also attending the end of season awards tonight. I normally bump into them on pre-season tours, which shows what fantastic support we have from the region.

As the girls had gone up to the White Hart to meet some of the Halifax lads, I headed into the ground in plenty of time to get in a good position for some photos. It was good to see the ground filling up but when fans were still clamouring for tickets, it was a shame to see the away part of the ground with plenty of spaces. It would have been nice to have kept the bottom tier for our fans, although I realise that with some disabled away fans, et cetera, this may have caused some issues. As I headed into the stand I'm glad I wasn't at the top of the stairs, as I'd have ended up with a stray ball on my head from the players practising shooting on the pitch! I did end up having a plastic beach ball land on my head when taking photos, though! Admittedly, that did have Laura in stitches when she saw it! The third thing was ending up with an elbow in my head when we scored later on, oh well, things do come in threes they say!

The team today was Green, Ayling, Berardi, Bartley, Jansson, Roofe, Hernandez, O'Kane, Wood, Dallas and Vieira. Subs were Doukara for Dallas, Pedraza for Ayling and Phillips for O'Kane. Attendance was 34,292 with approximately 1,000 Norwich fans. If I'd thought the singing in the Peacock moved me, then that was nothing in comparison to the 'Marching on Together' sung in the ground. With the full ground singing in unison, it was absolutely fantastic to hear. Before the game kicked off we had one minute's applause for all the Leeds fans that have died over the season, which was humbling.

My gut feelings were that we wouldn't make the play-offs but you never know in football. After having a conversation with a Huddersfield fan at work yesterday, I said that anyone can beat anyone in this division. I'd no idea how Norwich had been playing as of late but we were soon to find out. I didn't even realise that Jonny Howson, our ex-player, was in their team until I saw Norwich getting into the game more and more. His brother Danny travels with our branch to away games so he often chats about him. With 20 minutes on the clock, Norwich were making it look easy playing against us. I thought at that time that a single goal would seal the game. As Laura needed to go down to the toilets, I waited at the top of the stairs for her to come back. I had a good view then as another Norwich attack meant we didn't close them down and a long-range shot went hurling into the top of the net. I swore without realising but luckily the steward just smiled at me! When I went to find Laura, she said that she didn't want to come back and watch the game, which was an indication of how things were going on the pitch. We'd got back up to our seats when before we knew it we were two goals down. The reality at that time showed just how far away we are from going up and, to be honest, I didn't want to see this happen week in week out no matter how loyal a supporter I am! With Norwich nearly getting a third shortly afterwards it was tough to watch, then before long they did actually score to make it 3–0! With a minute of injury time on the clock we got an important goal when Wood seemed to be totally on his own with loads of space in the box, to put the ball into the net in front of the South Stand. Just before half-time meant we weren't totally down and out and could herald a comeback in the second half.

At half-time my daughter Michelle told Laura a song that she'd to sing. We're going to win 4–3! When we left to go back in the stands Margaret said that we'd go for the 4–3 then! Well, the team must have heard that too because we put up a tremendous fightback in the second half. Talk about a tale of two halves! As we attacked the goal in front of us from a Hernandez corner, Norwich looked to have cleared the ball off the line before Bartley put it into the net to send the Leeds fans into raptures. The volume at this time was deafening, and the thought of getting back into this game showed it was far from over.

Norwich started getting back into the game and Green denied them with a good couple of saves. With Leeds on the attack again, Berardi was brought down on the edge of the box and it took ages before the free-kick was taken. Berardi trying to get the ball off their time-wasting players got involved in an altercation that had a few handbags thrown about. From the resulting perfect free-kick from Hernandez the ball went sailing into the back of the net to equalise. Again, fantastic scenes as that 4–3 scoreline became a reality. As it was, Norwich nearly got that score when they came close. Despite them having a player sent off in the last couple of minutes plus six minutes injury time we had to settle for the draw.

I was really glad we had that fightback in the second half as it gave us something to believe in. If it had ended at half-time with the score 3–1 it would have been gutting. I'd had a few people come up to me today saying that they read my blogs and looked forward to reading them. All I can say is a big thank you to each and every one of you who does read them or have their photos taken. I write as a fan on behalf of fans everywhere of a football experience that takes us up and down the country following our team. The sacrifices many fans make is absolutely fantastic, and the things they have to do to follow Leeds at times is incredible. I must say I was so sorry to hear Brian Searson, who attends every Leeds game from Cornwall, couldn't make the game today despite having tickets. To hear his car had broken down was really sad to hear when so much effort is put into following Leeds. Laura enjoyed the second half and was cheering Leeds on. She also had her photos taken with some of the police and got the honour of wearing their hats! Talking of hats, she even pinched my beret at one point to be a mini me, but I was glad when I got it back as I realised it wasn't that warm!

Before the end of the game, Leeds had put a notice up on the screen, but I thought it was really bad PR when it said that anyone going onto the playing field would get an automatic one-year

ban. Now, fair enough, they want to keep fans off the pitch, but if we had achieved the play-offs today, denying everyone celebrating with the team is off in my opinion. Others may disagree but when I think back to our promotion against Bristol Rovers there were some fantastic scenes and celebrations that day on the pitch! We waited for the team to come around the pitch and we'd seen that Howson and Phillips had exchanged shirts. Howson then proceeded to come and clap the Kop and then the South Stand. You're Leeds and you know you are Jonny! At the end of the game I met up with my sister, niece and children at our usual meeting place at the crèche and stood for ages catching up. I wondered why the police horses started heading our way as we stood near Billy's statue but as usual I was oblivious to goings on, as I had missed the police escorting someone to one of the vans on Lowfields Road. I'm not sure what had happened for him to be arrested, but as it was long after the game had ended there hadn't really been anything going on along Elland Road that I could see. After Laura had further photos taken with the police when she told them that someone had been arrested, she said this had been the best day of her life! Out of the mouths of babes, as they say! Different reasons for some of us, though.

Listening to BBC Radio Leeds on the way home with Monk and Bartley being interviewed, it was telling that both said they'd had no contact from the club regarding contracts. Bartley was saying that he was still a Swansea player, but would not stay anyway if Monk wasn't here. Radrizzani's potential 100% takeover is completing on 1 June 2017, which is when we will know what direction the club is taking. What we have achieved this season has been fantastic compared with those of late and we have to build on this. Monk and players like Bartley and Jansson for starters are required for us to move on and have a good chance of automatic promotion next season. We cannot have no continuity and start again, as we have done nearly every year over the past few years. We need to build to give us a chance, and now is the time for the club to show that they believe in that vision too. For too long Leeds fans have been used as a cash cow for their fantastic loyalty and now need to see some return on that loyalty. As we are now mathematically not going into the play-offs, the 14,500 season ticket holders including myself who renewed before end of May last year will get refunds of 25%. The club, who hadn't sent out the forms needed to claim this back, despite saying they had to be back at the club by tomorrow, the 30 April deadline, said they will deal with them next week. Apparently they had been forgotten with us being in a play-off place for so long! I will take them at their word as long as this is forthcoming, and woe betide there are any problems with fans getting this refund. I'm sure it will all work out fine in the long run though. Some of us, including myself, have already renewed our season tickets for next year despite not knowing whether the refunds would be forthcoming or not.

Next week sees our final day at the early kick-off away game at Wigan. Despite everything being over for promotion, I am looking forward to a great day out with other Leeds fans. Our fans are what makes this club and this is the first team for ages, under Monk, that has given us belief again and connected us with the club. This is the basis for moving on, with a team that gets it and are proud to play for Leeds and know what it means to the fans. It's over to the club now to get it too! As Bartley said in his interview, onwards and upwards, see you next week LUFC – Marching on Together!

CHAPTER 11 – MAY 2017

WIGAN – 7 MAY 2017

I left home with the sun shining, only to arrive at a very cold and windy Elland Road. I'd also passed four individual magpies too, so thought that wouldn't be such a bad omen for the result today. I hung my banner around Billy's ankles to take some photos and wanted to climb up and drape it over his shoulders but thought better of it. Thinking about it, a woman of my age climbing on Billy's statue wouldn't be a pretty sight, plus knowing me I'd have fallen off! Our stop was at Leyland today and it didn't take us long to get there. Ours was the only coach there and we had a quiet couple of hours before leaving. When we arrived, though, the landlady spoke to our organiser to say he had to take personal responsibility for all our members. Apparently yesterday they'd had West Brom fans in, four coaches in total but only two booked in, who had caused all sorts of problems. We were already booked in for today and the police had been informed that we were coming. Thank you to Georgina for her support by buying my book *Follow Me and Leeds United*, unfortunately I didn't see Richard in the crowd at Wigan so will arrange something else. As usual, though, there were no issues with our members, who enjoy something to eat and drink on the way to a game.

Wigan A 7.5.17

Wigan A 7.5.17

We got to the ground at 11.15 a.m. for the 12.00 p.m. kick-off and found it in glorious sunshine, a complete contrast to Elland Road this morning. I went and hung my banner behind the goal and thought having my boots on maybe wasn't such a good idea, as the sun was cracking the flags at that point. As it was, my seat was further up the stand so I was in the shade so it didn't become an issue, although I stayed nearer the front for the second half.

The team today was Green, Bartley, Berardi, Coyle, Ayling, O'Kane, Roofe, Dallas, Wood, Hernandez and Vieira. Subs were Pedraza for Hernandez, Sacko for Dallas and Phillips for Vieira. Attendance was 15,280 with 4,720 Leeds fans. Either Wigan had loads of fans who stayed away due to them already being relegated, or it was the amount of Leeds fans in the home side to the

Wigan A 7.5.17

Wigan A 7.5.17

Wigan A 7.5.17

right of us who swelled the crowd. Looking at my photos, though, I cannot believe they had more fans in total in the three sides than the Leeds fans in our stand!

With nothing to play for (despite me saying only 14–0 would do – tongue in cheek, lol!) I wasn't expecting very much from the game, which proved to be. Ayling was playing centre back in place of Jansson who was suspended and he didn't look too comfortable in that position during the first half. Wigan had started off brightly and within six minutes were ahead, when they got into the penalty area and had a clear shot of goal. 15–1, the Leeds fans sang, but as we thought, the margins of scoring so many were not going to happen. Monk had the support of the Leeds fans saying we had to sign him up! It wasn't long after that when I realised that the stewards in the stand to the right of me were getting all the Leeds fans in there to come to the end of the stand nearest to us. There was plenty of banter between the two sets of Leeds fans then. A couple of Wigan fans were kicking off, but were spoken to by a steward and backed off. As least it was good to see it hadn't descended into the free-for-all that happened at Blackpool a couple of seasons ago.

The first half didn't offer much more to be honest, and I was starting to flag by half-time and was glad there were only a couple of minutes of injury time. The second half meant we started off brighter and it was good to see Ayling make some runs forward and look threatening. He looked more comfortable in the position he was playing too. We started playing forward a lot more and when O'Kane was brought down in the penalty area that was the cue for Wood to take the penalty for his 30th goal of the season. It was quite an even game after this, where we had a shot off the crossbar and Wigan had a chance where Green parried the shot and Bartley helped to clear the ball behind him.

Wigan A 7.5.17

At the end of the game the players and staff came to applaud all the Leeds fans and as they looked in awe at the support, I personally don't think they will ever see that from other fans. As a club, Leeds United are very lucky that they have the loyal support that they have.

It was good to get back to Elland Road in good time due to the early kick-off, although I couldn't believe it was back to an icy biting wind once more and no sun! At least it was better weather back in Halifax.

That's the end of this season now, and we will shortly hear about the takeover with Radrizzani gaining 100%. I am optimistic but am keeping my eyes and ears open, because as Leeds fans we have had so much to put up with over the years. I will see what happens and judge on what I see.

It won't be long before the fixtures are out for next season and we are back again. I hope everyone has chance to relax before we start again. Personally, I have a busy time ahead with my youngest daughter's wedding and plenty of family things to do.

Enjoy the close season and see you in July when our warm-up starts once again! LUFC – Marching on Together!

Wigan A 7.5.17

FIXTURES FOR THE SEASON 2016–17

Date	Opposition	Venue	Competition	Score	Att	Scorers
16/07/2016	Shamrock Rovers	Tallaght Stadium, Dublin	Pre-Season Friendly	0-3	4,000 approx	Antonsson (2) Wood (Penalty)
22/07/2016	Guiseley	Nethermoor Park	Pre-Season Friendly	3-4	2,433	Stokes Botaka Phillips Doukara
30/07/2016	Atalanta	Elland Road	Pre-Season Friendly	2-1	11,832	Wood Roofe
7/08/2016	Qpr	Loftus Road	Championship	3-0	16,674	
10/08/2016	Fleetwood	Highbury Stadium	Efl Cup 1St Round	2-2	3,332	Antonsson Wood Leeds Won On Penalties Wood Antonsson Mowatt Phillips Hernandez
13/08/2016	Birmingham	Elland Road	Championship	1-2	12,236	Sacko
16/08/2016	Fulham	Elland Road	Championship	1-1	12,279	Wood
20/08/2016	Sheffield Wednesday	Hillsborough	Championship	0-2	29,075	Antonsson Wood
23/08/2016	Luton	Kenilworth Road	Efl Cup 2Nd Round	0-1	7,498 1,510 Leeds Fans	Denton
27/08/2016	Nottingham Forest	City Ground	Championship	3-1	20,995 With 1,925 Leeds Fans	Phillips
10/09/2016	Huddersfield	Elland Road	Championship	0-1	28,514 2,721 Huddersfield Fans	
13/09/2016	Blackburn	Elland Road	Championship	2-1	19,009 327 Blackburn Fans	Wood Bartley
17/09/2016	Cardiff	Cardiff City Stadium	Championship	0-2	16,608 Approx 2,000 Leeds Fans	Wood Hernandez
20/09/2016	Blackburn	Elland Road	Efl Cup 3Rd Round	1-0	8,488 463 Blackburn Fans	Wood
24/09/2016	Ipswich	Elland Road	Championship	1-0	22,554 902 Ipswich Fans	Wood
27/09/2016	Bristol City	Ashton Gate	Championship	1-0	19,699 2,065 Leeds Fans	
01/10/2016	Barnsley	Elland Road	Championship	2-1	27,350 2,413 Barnsley Fans	Bartley Hernandez

Date	Opposition	Venue	Competition	Score	Att	Scorers
15/10/2016	Derby	Pride Park Stadium	Championship	1-0	31,170 3,132 Leeds Fans	
18/10/2016	Wigan	Elland Road	Championship	1-1	19,861 400 Wigan Fans	Wood
22/10/2016	Wolverhampton Wanderers	Molineux Stadium	Championship	0-1	23,607 2,452 Leeds Fans	Silvio o.g.
25/10/2016	Norwich	Elland Road	Efl Cup 4Th Round	2-2	22,222	Antonsson Wood Leeds Win On Penalties Wood Roofe Vieira (3-2 Penalties)
29/10/2016	Burton Albion	Elland Road	Championship	2-0	24,220 500 Burton Fans	Wood Doukara
5/11/2016	Norwich	Carrow Road	Championship	2-3	26,903 Approx 3,000 Leeds Fans	Jansson Wood Vieira
20/11/2016	Newcastle	Elland Road	Championship	0-2	36,002 2,700 Newcastle Fans	
26/11/20/16	Rotherham	New York Stadium	Championship	1-2	10,513 2,277 Leeds Fans	Wood Doukara
29/11/16	Liverpool	Anfield	Efl Cup 5Th Round	2-0	52,012 5,352 Leeds Fans	
03/12/2016	Aston Villa	Elland Road	Championship	2-0	32,648 Approx 3,000 Villa Fans	Roofe Wood
09/12/2016	Brighton	Falmer Stadium	Championship	2-0	28,206 2,736 Leeds Fans	
13/12/2016	Reading	Elland Road	Championship	2-0	21,242 Approx 200 Reading Fans	Wood Doukara (Pen)
17/12/2016	Brentford	Elland Road	Championship	1-0	25,134 Approx 200 Brentford Fans	Bartley
26/12/2016	Preston	Deepdale	Championship	1-4	21,255 Approx 5,700 Leeds Fans	Roofe Sacko Doukara Hernandez
29/12/2016	Aston Villa	Villa Park	Championship	1-1	37,078 Approx 3,000 Leeds Fans	Jansson
02/01/2017	Rotherham	Elland Road	Championship	3-0	33,397	Wood (2) Bartley

Date	Opposition	Venue	Competition	Score	Att	Scorers
09/01/2017	Cambridge	Abbey Stadium	Fa Cup 3Rd Round	1-2	7,973 1,414 Leeds Fans	Dallas Mowatt
13/01/2017	Derby	Elland Road	Championship	1-0	25,546 Approx 1,000 Derby Fans	Wood
21/01/2017	Barnsley	Oakwell	Championship	3-2	17,817 5,241 Leeds	Wood (2) (1 Pen)
25/01/2017	Nottingham Forest	Elland Road	Championship	2-0	24,838 Approx. 500 Forest	Wood Doukara
29/01/2017	Sutton United	Gander Green Lane	Fa Cup 4Th Round	1-0	4,997 Approx 774 Leeds Fans	
01/02/2017	Blackburn	Ewood Park	Championship	1-2	17,026 6,402 Leeds Fans	Dallas Jansson
05/02/2017	Huddersfield	Kirklees Stadium	Championship	2-1	22,400 1,958 Leeds Fans	Wood
11/02/2017	Cardiff	Elland Road	Championship	0-2	31,516	
14/02/2017	Bristol City	Elland Road	Championship	2-1	22,402 Approx 300 Bristol Fans	Wood Hernandez
18/02/2017	Ipswich Town	Portman Road	Championship	1-1	18,745 2,113 Leeds Fans	Dallas
25/02/2017	Sheffield Wednesday	Elland Road	Championship	1-0	35,093 Approx 2,800 Wednesday Fans	Wood
03/03/2017	Birmingham	St Andrews	Championship	1-3	20,321 Approx 3,000 Leeds Fans	Wood (2) Pedraza
07/03/2017	Fulham	Craven Cottage	Championship	1-1	22,239 7,200 Leeds Fans	Og
11/03/2017	Qpr	Elland Road	Championship	0-0	30,870 870 Qpr Fans	
18/03/2017	Brighton	Elland Road	Championship	2-0	29,767 Approx. 1,500 Brighton Fans	Wood (2)
01/04/2017	Reading	Madejski Stadium	Championship	1-0	23,055 3,546 Leeds Fans	
04/04/2017	Brentford	Griffin Park	Championship	2-0	10,759 Approx 1,700 Leeds Fans	
08/04/2017	Preston	Elland Road	Championship	3-0	31,851 Approx 1,800 Preston Fans	Roofe Hernandez Doukara
14/04/2017	Newcastle	St James Park	Championship	1-1	52,301 Approx 3,000 Leeds Fans	Wood

Date	Opposition	Venue	Competition	Score	Att	Scorers
17/04/2017	Wolverhampton Wanderers	Elland Road	Championship	0-1	32,351 Approx 1,000 Wolves Fans	
22/04/2017	Burton Albion	Pirelli Stadium	Championship	2-1	6,073 Approx 1,600 Leeds Fans	Bartley
29/04/2017	Norwich	Elland Road	Championship	3-3	34,292 Approx 1,000 Norwich Fans	Wood Bartley Hernandez
07/05/2017	Wigan	Dw Stadium	Championship	1-1	15,280 4,720 Leeds Fans	Wood (Pen)

CHAMPIONSHIP TABLE 2016–17

	P	W	D	L	F	A	GD	PTS
NEWCASTLE UNITED	46	29	7	10	85	40	45	94
BRIGHTON	46	28	9	9	74	40	34	93
READING FC	46	26	7	13	68	64	4	85
SHEFFIELD WEDNESDAY	46	24	9	13	60	45	15	81
HUDDERSFIELD TOWN	46	25	6	15	56	58	-2	81
FULHAM	46	22	14	10	85	57	28	80
LEEDS UNITED	46	22	9	15	61	47	14	75
NORWICH CITY	46	20	10	16	85	69	16	70
DERBY COUNTY	46	18	13	15	54	50	4	67
BRENTFORD	46	18	10	18	75	65	10	64
PRESTON	46	16	14	16	64	63	1	62
CARDIFF CITY	46	17	11	18	60	61	-1	62
ASTON VILLA	46	16	14	16	47	48	-1	62
BARNSLEY	46	15	13	18	64	67	-3	58
WOLVERHAMPTON WANDERERS	46	16	10	20	54	58	-4	58
IPSWICH TOWN	46	13	16	17	48	58	-10	55
BRISTOL CITY	46	15	9	22	60	66	-6	54
QUEENS PARK RANGERS	46	15	8	23	52	66	-14	53
BIRMINGHAM CITY	46	13	14	19	45	64	-19	53
BURTON ALBION	46	13	13	20	49	63	-14	52
NOTTINGHAM FOREST	46	14	9	23	62	72	-10	51
BLACKBURN ROVERS (R)	46	12	15	19	53	65	-12	51
WIGAN (R)	46	10	12	24	40	57	-17	42
ROTHERHAM UNITED (R)	46	5	8	33	40	98	−58	23

CHAPTER 12 –

LOOKING FORWARD: WHERE DO WE GO NEXT?

Now the season has ended and we know we are in the Championship again next season, my feelings are that we should go for automatic promotion next season. Personally, I would much rather go up that way than go through the play-offs as it is too stressful. Today has seen the final team Huddersfield promoted that way and we now know who we up against in the division. As I said this year, anyone could beat anyone on the day and this is what has transpired most of the season. The two teams who went up automatically, Newcastle and Brighton, probably were the most consistent though.

I was also looking forward to some stability, as we have just had Radrizzani completing his 100% purchase of Leeds United from Cellino. With Monk in situ, I thought things were looking good that way. Wrong! After Leeds activated the clause of an extension to Monk's contract he decided to resign, and so we go back to square once again at this moment in time. I found I wasn't as upset as I thought I'd be, and realised that my friend Sue had been right as for some reason she didn't take to Monk. What I still cannot understand to this day, though, is as he has resigned and maybe was going to in any case, why he threw Charlie Taylor under a bus on the last game of the season at Wigan? There has been plenty of stuff thrown at Taylor from the Leeds fans because of 'his refusal to play', whereas I found myself thinking at the time that there had to be more to it? Taylor was due to leave the club, he hadn't been included in a meeting at the start of the week apparently, and as far as I am aware hadn't been training as his season was over. Why Monk suddenly decided he wanted Charlie to play that last Sunday was a mystery to me despite Cooper's injury? He could have tried some of the young ones in the team who were on the fringes to give them a chance to play? I have heard rumours that Charlie had been injured and maybe we will never know the real truth, but my gut feelings told me it wasn't all as portrayed. Was it deflection as we hadn't got to the play-offs and to let someone else get the blame? Who knows, but I still think that there was no reason for this to happen in the first place. With Monk doing exactly what he accused Taylor of doing last week, then I'm afraid it leaves a bad taste in my mouth!

From what I heard later, Charlie had indeed been playing with an injury. His Achilles injury earlier in the season meant he played with injections to ensure he could play. Whilst Leeds were in with a chance of the play-offs he was to play, but once there was no chance of promotion he was to be given time to get over the injury, hence why he didn't play today. I'm afraid I don't believe the spin that came out of the club that day putting all the blame on Charlie either, as my gut reactions told me differently, sadly.

There have been plenty of things going on behind the scenes, since the end of the season, with the ground having been brought back by Radrizzani. I'll admit that this brought tears to my eyes as I was so happy. We have a new manager in Thomas Christiansen and have been putting in place a backroom team, including a scouting network. Recruitment of players for both the first team and the academy have also been made. We need to get off to a good start with any potential new faces in the team as soon as we can, to ensure they can gel as early as possible. Our pre-season plans were announced very late but Leeds fans who travel everywhere still followed them abroad. The loyalty of the fans means they will be there regardless and I am hopeful the club will be in a good position to reciprocate this for once.

Having been interviewed for a new season ticket video, I was overwhelmed to see this had over 50,000 views on LUTV. I have also been on *Made in Leeds – All Leeds Aren't We* as part of a quiz team (I didn't expect to get any answers right, by the way) and had a late-night interview on BBC Five Live recently. I know plenty of times I can be seen waffling but it is nice that others want me to take part in things. Although I am aware other fans will have a different opinion to me and they are entitled to it, I will always say how I see things from a personal point of view. My support of Leeds United cannot be questioned, as I am still loyal to them having supported them for over 50 years. Having had the privilege of seeing the best team ever play under Don Revie, together with my hero Billy Bremner (he always was and always will be my hero), they are the reason I am the Leeds United supporter I am today. I have had a season ticket for approximately 30 years, as before that I got complimentary tickets into the ground through selling bingo cards, and have already renewed mine for next season. I have seen the good times and also the bad times but I wouldn't change it for the world. Being there to see things for myself has meant I have travelled the world following my team, and have met thousands of Leeds fans along the way. Our support many times has been the only thing that has kept me going to games but one thing is for sure, we will always be Marching on Together! See you next season!

ND - #0266 - 270225 - C0 - 234/156/15 - PB - 9781780915678 - Gloss Lamination